Hyphens & Hashtags

Hyphens & Hashtags*

The stories behind the symbols on our keyboards

Claire Cock-Starkey

Bodleian Library
UNIVERSITY OF OXFORD

First published in 2021 by the Bodleian Library
Broad Street, Oxford OX1 3BG
www.bodleianshop.co.uk

ISBN 978 1 85124 536 9

Cover design by Dot Little at the Bodleian Library
Designed and typeset in 11½ on 14 Bulmer by illuminati, Grosmont
Printed and bound by Livonia Print, Latvia,
on 115 gsm Munken Print Cream paper

MIX
Paper from
responsible sources
FSC® C002795
www.fsc.org

British Library Catalogue in Publishing Data
A CIP record of this publication is available from the British Library

Contents

The semicolon is far more common in the elder English Classics ... It was perhaps used in excess by them; but the disuse seems a worse evil.

Samuel Taylor Coleridge

Cut out all those exclamation marks. An exclamation mark is like laughing at your own jokes.

F. Scott Fitzgerald

Introduction

In an apocryphal story which first appeared in William S. Walsh's *Handy-book of Literary Curiosities* (1892), Victor Hugo was said to have instigated the most concise literary correspondence in history. On the publication of *Les Misérables* in 1862, Hugo was desperate to know how the book fared, so he sent his publisher a telegram reading simply: '?' The publisher, pleased that the book had sold over 6,000 copies in its first few days and was due for a reprint, replied with an emphatic '!' Although the veracity of this charming anecdote may be in doubt, it does neatly illustrate the power of special characters in conveying a concept succinctly. Those symbols, which haunt the margins of our keyboards, shape our understanding of texts, calculations and online interactions. Without punctuation, glyphs and mathematical symbols all texts would run in endless unbroken lines of letters and numbers.

The development of writing is dynamic. The way we communicate has evolved over the years from handwritten manuscripts mostly created for the devotion of God, through business records with their need for calculations, via the development of the printing press and the dawning of mass media, to the impact of high-speed digital communication. As our need to communicate in written form has grown and developed, so too have the symbols and glyphs which help us to express or clarify our meaning.

In this book I have attempted to trace the history of some of the most interesting and important symbols used in the English language (and commonly found on English-language keyboards). To do this I have grouped them into sections: punctuation, mathematical symbols, glyphs, endangered and extinct symbols. In this way readers might choose to dip in and out, each entry providing a complete potted history of the symbol in question. However, by reading the entire book the story behind the key characters on our keyboards can be pieced together and the themes which see some symbols triumph while others fall by the wayside can be appreciated.

The story of special characters is one of ebb and flow. Not every symbol has a linear route from invention to common usage. For many of the special characters included within this book there were a number of options vying for ascendancy, often in different regions. Some coexisted for hundreds of years; others saw their original meaning lost, only for them to be subbed in for another purpose – proving, at least, that you can't keep a good symbol down.

What has become clear to me as I have researched this book is that often it was not the original writer of a work who decided on a symbol, but the scribe who was copying their words. Likewise, as the printing press developed it was frequently the typesetter who selected which symbol would be cast into type and therefore thrust into popular usage. In the literary world it was often editors and proofreaders who shaped how a text would reach the public, much to the chagrin of writers such as Mark Twain, who over the course of his writing career was constantly railing against changes made to his original manuscripts by editors. In 1897 he wrote to his publisher Chatto & Windus: 'I give it up. These printers pay no attention to my punctuation. Nine-tenths of the labor & vexation put upon me by Messrs. Spottiswoode & Co consists in annihilating their ignorant & purposeless punctuation &

restoring my own."* And so the story of many special characters' route into common usage reflects the dynamic development of writing and the many hands that play a role in selecting and refining the end product of a printed book or article.

As I was writing *Hyphens & Hashtags* I was aware that I was describing something, especially in the realms of punctuation, which can have multiple uses and meanings depending on the context. This is never truer than in the digital age, where restricted word counts, informality and activism have all impacted on how we use punctuation online. Although emoji have served to gift us a plethora of ways to communicate in symbol form, many traditional pieces of punctuation have been creatively reimagined online to convey fresh meanings – from the correcting flair of an asterisk to the warmth bestowed by a bracketed (((hug))). In this way I have tried to follow the latest developments of the many symbols considered in this book, but I appreciate that it is inevitable that this is an area which continues to grow and develop, and that is what makes the role of special characters so endlessly fascinating.

* Mark Twain, letter to his publisher Chatto & Windus in 1897, as quoted in *Letters of Note*, ed. Shaun Usher, Canongate, Edinburgh, 2013.

Punctuation

A comma does nothing but make easy
a thing that if you like it enough is easy enough
without the comma.

Gertrude Stein, *Lectures in America*, 1935

Punctuation was not inherent to the development of writing. It did not formalize or regularize until many hundreds of years after written languages were first created. It was not until the 1660s that the word 'punctuation' began to mean the system of adding pauses into written works, and this perhaps reflects its very slow creep (with numerous tangential trips down dark alleys) on its long journey towards the system we recognize today.

To understand the history of punctuation we must first understand the development of written English. In antiquity texts were read aloud and so writing was a reflection of the spoken word. This meant that its conventions differed from our modern formal mode of writing. Latin – which was originally written entirely in upper case with no spaces between the words – was the language of the scriptures, and so Latin became the language of religion, scholarship and government. The arrival of

Christianity and its emphasis on written scripture was hugely influential in the development of the concept of punctuation. The clarity of God's message became increasingly important, and early punctuation marks served as a visual clue to help the reader understand how the text should be read aloud, for example by indicating pauses. By the eighth century CE, English and Irish scribes had at last begun to copy texts with spaces between the words to make Latin easier to decipher for non-native speakers, a development which made reading a less onerous task and created space that punctuation could fill.

Charlemagne, king of the Franks commissioned the creation of a more user-friendly script around 780 CE. Featuring lower-case letters and spaces between words, it became known as 'Carolingian minuscule'. At the end of the ninth century, King Alfred the Great promoted Christianity in England by encouraging the translation of Latin religious texts into English so that they might be more widely read. These incremental changes to writing practices slowly served to make reading more accessible, and punctuation more essential. However, when scribes were copying texts by hand, punctuation marks could differ wildly depending on space, whim and the potential to embellish. This led to a whole host of different marks being used across Europe to indicate pauses of varying lengths. Some order was introduced by humanist writers in the thirteenth and fourteenth centuries. They employed a greater amount of punctuation because communicating their ideas with precision had become increasingly important in this new culture of intellectual thought. Yet still various different marks were used and each writer often had their own system, meaning that there was still no accepted standard.

The development of the printing press in the fifteenth century had a huge impact on punctuation – books were not only becoming cheaper and quicker to produce but more widely read too. Type cutters needed to hand craft each individual letter or mark, and so each symbol was carefully considered before being committed to print. At first each printer used their own system, largely based on handwritten scripts, but, as more and more books were produced and with larger circulation, greater standardization and simplification crept in as the printed word became distinct from handwritten, cursive script. By the sixteenth century, specialist type founders such as Claude Garamond (*c.* 1490–1561) had become established, meaning that most printers, rather than cutting their own distinct type, would buy typefaces from larger suppliers. This further solidified the appearance of punctuation, although its practical usage remained largely undefined.

The first English grammar guide was *Pamphlet for Grammar* (1586) by printer William Bullokar. This attempted to codify the rules of writing the English language; however, it still clung to the rules of Latin and was heavily based on William Lily's *Latin Grammar* (*c.* 1540). In 1542 Lily's work was the only book on Latin grammar authorized by Henry VIII to be taught in English schools. It was to be the foremost book on grammar for hundreds of years, being widely used right up to the nineteenth century, ensuring Latin ideas of grammar were instilled into generations of English schoolchildren.

Modern English punctuation was largely set by *The King's English* (1906), a book on grammar and usage by brothers Henry Watson Fowler and Francis George Fowler. The book was a huge success and ushered in an era of less-is-more when it comes to marks on the page, promoting a sparer use of punctuation than had been popular in the eighteenth and nineteenth centuries.

Language and grammar are ever evolving; this is especially true in the age of the Internet, where punctuation has in some cases seen a reduction in use (think full stops), and in others an inflation (think exclamation marks). In the world of punctuation, things are never set in stone.

Full stop

The full stop (or period if you are American) is one of the most basic, commonly used and essential pieces of punctuation as it indicates finality, with the end of a sentence. As you would expect with such a vital piece of punctuation, it was one of the first formal marks to be developed and recognized, but as with all punctuation its route into common usage was not without dead ends and wrong turns.

The first appearance of the 'dot' in writing came in the sixth century CE as monks began to copy out Latin religious texts. This shift from passing down stories and religious works orally to the Christian need to preserve the written word was key to the development of modern writing in the West. Roman texts were written in capitals with no punctuation and no spaces between words. This was slow and cumbersome to copy and extremely difficult to read. The monks, keen to speed up the copying of texts, developed small (minuscule), cursive (Latin for 'running') or joined-up writing, which meant their quill need not leave the page. This was all very well for the speed of writing but it made reading even slower as the words all melded into one. To correct this, some monks began separating each word with a dot, which helped those reading aloud to follow the text more easily. However, there was still the problem of separating out ideas or indicating the end of a thought – in rhetoric known as a *periodus* – and so the monks began using a group of three dots together to mark the close of a sentence. By the seventh century, Irish and Scottish monks had dispensed with the dot between words, realizing that a space worked just as well and required no ink. At the same time the system of three dots, first introduced by Aristophanes in the third century BCE, came back into fashion as Isidore of Seville (560–636 CE) popularized their usage, with the high dot, or *distinctio finalis*, serving to close a sentence. Dots, then, were serving the purpose of a variety of modern punctuation symbols; their usage was erratic and differed according to the individual scribe. As minuscule letters became more commonly used, the distinction between high, low and middle dots became harder to determine and so most dots now found their way down to the baseline.

And so it was that, with the introduction of the printing press in the fifteenth century, typographers had a plethora of dots from which to choose. William Caxton began printing books in London in 1476. Although he experimented with a few different marks, he ultimately decided on the slash, or solidus, to group words together; the colon to show synaptic pauses; the full stop to show both a short pause and the end of a sentence. As the impact of the printing press was felt and books could now be produced more quickly and circulated more widely, reading, writing, punctuation and spelling began to become more regularized, and the full stop was one of the earliest punctuation marks to gain a clear and consistent meaning. Francis Bacon's *Essays* (1597) can be said to be one of the first books in English to show 'modern' punctuation, and it was during this period that a wider consensus on the use of a full stop to mark the end of a sentence grew, its previous role as short pause between words being taken by other distinct marks.

The dot had been known under various names, but come the sixteenth century, as teachers began to explain to their pupils the difference between the half stop of the comma and the full stop of the end of a sentence, the English name 'full stop' was arrived at. The dot also retained its Latin name, 'period'. This was originally a grammatical term that referred to a complete sentence, the end of which was indicated by the dot that now carries this name. The word 'period' remained interchangeable with 'full stop' until the nineteenth century when the British began to favour the latter and Americans the former.

The dot today has a number of different names and uses. As a period it can be used to indicate the contraction to initials in a name such as A.A. Milne (although some modern English style guides eschew this usage). Traditionally a dot was also used to indicate the contraction of a long word to a shorter one. However, again the English and the Americans diverged, with English style guides ruling that a dot should only be employed for a shortening such as Prof. (for Professor), whereas American guides also recommend a dot for contractions such as Mr. and Dr. In mathematics the dot has a different name, 'decimal point', and is used to delineate between a whole number and the fractional part, as in 2.5.

With the age of the Internet the full stop has gained yet another usage and name: the dot without spaces is used to separate out Internet and email addresses. It is interesting to note that although the Internet has given the full stop a further job, the age of instant messaging has also seen a decline in its use. Short text messages tend to offer no punctuation at all (save for the liberal use of emoji), with a line break often used to indicate the end of a sentence. This informal, chatty style is so common in text-speak that the use of a full stop can now be read as an aggressive or assertive addition to a message, communicating a definite finality.

Comma

Today the comma is the most commonly used punctuation mark in English, attesting to its importance in improving the clarity of written English. Many people still subscribe to the advice to place a comma wherever you would take a breath, which today would be considered overkill. However, this advice traces the root of the comma back to its origins as an aid to reading devotional texts aloud. Initially scribes used a dot over the word to indicate where a breath should be taken, and this came to form the early concept of a comma. In the twelfth century Italian scholar Boncompagno da Signa began using the slash (also known as a solidus, and as *virgula suspensive* or virgule; see page 81) in place of the middle dot as a comma, and the clarity of this symbol meant it soon caught on.

The dawn of the printing press saw a number of marks competing for the role of comma. William Caxton came down on the side of the slash and used this in his early English printings from 1476. However, humanist scholar Aldus Manutius, recognized as the best printer in Venice in the 1490s, eschewed the virgule, instead inventing a new symbol: the semi-circular comma we would recognize today. Such was the beauty and simplicity of this new symbol that its use soon spread north with humanist scholarship and it began appearing in English texts from 1520. Initially in many documents a mixture of commas and virgules were used to do the same job, but ultimately Manutius' symbol saw off its competitors and became the standard mark for a comma.

So the shape of the comma had been decided, but its usage was still undefined. This set the stage for a debate, still ongoing, over how we use the humble comma. In the English language excessive punctuation was rife in the eighteenth century, with commas littering every sentence, which often ran on and on. Order was called in 1906 with the publication of Henry Watson Fowler and Francis George Fowler's *The King's English*. This hugely influential book pushed the case for light punctuation, a mantle that most modern writers are happy to take up.

The comma, though, has remained a controversial piece of punctuation with the ongoing bitter disagreement over the usage of the serial comma, also known as the Oxford comma. It is thought that the rules of the serial comma were first laid down by Horace Hart, printer at Oxford University Press, who published his style guide for the press, *Hart's Rules for Compositors and Readers at the University Press Oxford* in 1905. In it he stressed that when writing a list there should be a comma after the last word before 'and'. This apocryphal book dedication ably illustrates his point: 'This book is dedicated to my parents, Ayn Rand and God' – without the serial comma it reads as if the author's parents are Ayn Rand and God. With the serial comma the true meaning is clear: 'This book is dedicated to my parents, Ayn Rand, and God'. The serial comma did not become known as the Oxford comma until 1978 when Peter Sutcliffe dubbed it that in his book on the history of the Oxford University Press. With the current trend for light punctuation, the Oxford comma is seen as superfluous by many. Major style guides such as that of the Associated Press advise against its use, except in cases where a sentence could be misinterpreted without one. Indeed the house style for the publisher of this book, the Bodleian Library, does not subscribe to the Oxford comma, so with the exception of the example above you will not find one in this book. *The Chicago Manual of Style*, however, still recommends the use of the Oxford comma. So it seems that this is one debate that will continue.

Colon

The word 'colon' derives from the Greek *kōlon*, meaning 'limb'. This origin indicates how the colon was perceived as separating the sections, or limbs, of a sentence into clauses. The colon, like most other modern punctuation marks, has its roots in classical Greek writings. These works were originally written as continuous lines of text in majuscule script (like modern capital letters) with no spaces between words or letters, making them very difficult to read aloud. Aristophanes of Byzantium, the librarian at Alexandria, has been credited with introducing a system of dots in the third century BCE to clarify writing and indicate to the reader where to pause or take a breath. A short section was indicated by a central dot after the last word of the section, and this became known as a *comma*. Aristophanes' *colon* was used to indicate the end of a longer section and was represented by what today we would recognize as a full stop. The pause after the longest section was shown with a *periodos*, which was a single dot at the end of the section at the top of the final letter.

In the seventh century Archbishop Isidore of Seville added greater definition to Aristophanes' system, tying meanings to each of the three dots. The low dot he termed *subdistinctio*, using it as we do a modern comma for a short pause. The middle dot he named *media distinctio*; this he used somewhat like a colon. The high dot he termed a *distinctio finalis*, and this served as a full stop to mark the end of a sentence. These marks were still largely to indicate how to read a passage aloud. The middle dot was used as an in-between mark, longer than the short pause of a comma (or low dot) but shorter than the more definite end point offered by the full stop (or high dot). This midpoint was likely how the colon went on to develop as a way of dividing a sentence into independent clauses.

The eighth century saw the Carolingians introduce greater clarity to Latin texts with the use of lower-case letters developed by Alcuin of York (*c.* 735–804). However, the range of punctuation marks used and their meanings still differed, with many scribes using their own system. One possible origin of the modern colon shape is medieval scribes, who began borrowing the marks from Gregorian chants that were used to indicate pauses in devotional songs. The *punctus elevatus*, which resembled an upside-down semicolon, was thus adopted by some writings in the fourteenth century. Over time the tail of the upper part of the mark disappeared, leaving the two dots of a modern colon.

With the introduction of the printing press in the fifteenth century, scribes' marks became formalized as the symbols we recognize today but their meanings were not yet defined or set. English printer William Caxton, who set up his printing shop in London in 1476, experimented with a number of punctuation marks but soon settled on just three: the slash (/) to indicate groups of words; the colon (:) to show pauses in the syntax; and the full stop (.) to indicate pauses or the end of a sentence. Caxton's success meant that his system of punctuation was widely seen; however, numerous contemporary printers were employing other marks and meanings and so no consensus of usage was reached.

It seems likely that it was George Puttenham who first used the word 'colon' in English in his *The Arte of English Poesie* (1589). Puttenham adopted the Latin term (itself from Greek origin) as a way to describe the length of pauses when reading poetry aloud – the comma being the shortest pause and the colon being twice as long. This punctuation, however, was purely elocutionary and not used to clarify syntax as it is today. It was not until the eighteenth century that the modern usage of the colon began to be set, although there remained plenty of variants. The colon kept its medieval role as a sort of middle dot, splitting a sentence into two main clauses; for example, 'The dog had one main hobby: it slept.' It also began to be used before speech marks and as a method of separating a book or article title into the main title and subtitle; for example, *Oliver Twist: The Parish Boy's Progress.* The colon is also used to indicate the start of a list; for example, 'The dog had a number of hobbies: eating, sleeping and chasing sticks.'

Numerically the colon is used to denote ratio, as in 10:1, but also to indicate a Bible verse, thus Genesis 1:1. In America it is used when writing the time, 12:15 p.m., whereas in Britain a dot is used, 12.15 p.m. Americans also use a colon at the start of a formal letter, 'Dear Sir:', where British practice is to use a comma. Today the colon is used infrequently in everyday writing, the shorter sentences favoured by Millennials seemingly less in need of the colon's help. Today, in informal writing in the digital age, a frequent deployment of the colon is to shortcut to the smiling-face emoji thus :) by placing a colon in front of a right-hand bracket. The colon may no longer be adding much to the structure of our writing, but its new role as the eyes of a happy face is at least adding some warmth to our online communications.

Semicolon

Italian printer Aldus Manutius (1449–1515) set up his Aldine Press in Venice in 1494. At that time Venice was one of the richest cities in Europe, and many artists and artisans made their home there as the arts flourished during the Renaissance. Manutius was an innovator, and many of his advances in printing had a profound effect on both punctuation and the history of the book. It was Manutius who developed a method to print the Greek script, meaning that works in Ancient Greek could reach a much wider audience. Furthermore, as enormous folios were unwieldy, he realized that if a Bible folio page was folded over, in half, quarters and finally eighths, it created a smaller, more portable book, which became known as an octavo. As books became smaller, legible typefaces and clear punctuation became increasingly important. Consequently, Manutius worked with the best type cutters, including Francesco Griffo, who in 1500 first used an italic typeface in Manutius's edition of Virgil.

The Aldine Press published Dante's *Divine Comedy* and Erasmus' *Adagia*, as well as works by Ancient Greek and Latin writers such as Catullus, Sophocles, Plato and Herodotus. While developing these smaller editions Manutius recognized that punctuation needed to be modified in order to aid the reader to read the text silently in their head, as opposed to aloud as was traditional. As a result he felt that there needed to be a punctuation mark which fell somewhere between a full stop and a comma. In Pietro Bembo's *De Aetna*, an account of the ascent of Mount Etna published in 1494, Manutius employed a colon with the bottom dot replaced by a comma, as a way to separate items in a list, much as today we might use a comma. This was the first ever instance of a semicolon in print. But where did the mark come from?

It seems likely that Manutius was inspired by the hand-drawn punctuation marks used by medieval scribes. One such mark was the *punctus versus*, which looks remarkably similar to the semicolon. This mark had its roots in the musical notation which had been used to copy down Gregorian chants, and its use indicated a long pause or break in the text. Italian scholars soon adopted the semi-colon, and its usage spread northwards to humanist scholars and printers across Europe. It is thought English printer Henry Denham was the first to adopt Manutius's use of the semicolon in an English work, in the 1580s, and Ben Jonson cemented its use by including it in his guide to the writing and pronunciation of English, *The English Grammar* (1640).

Use of the semicolon became more widespread across Europe, peaking with the fashionably long sentences of eighteenth-century writers; English writers in particular found it a good way to separate clauses without the finality of a full stop. The use of the semicolon has remained contentious and subject to fashion. In February 1837 things came to a head when the *Standard* reported that two French jurisconsults of the Law School in Paris had engaged in a duel with short swords over the issue. The row arose over the Pandects (a compendium of Roman laws), with one asserting that the passage in question ought to close with a semicolon, while the other, quoting eminent Roman lawyer Trebonius, insisted it should be a colon. The duel was decided in favour of the colon when the semicolon supporter was wounded in the arm, but this decisive victory did little to settle the correct usage of the semicolon in the wider world.

Textual analysis by Paul Bruthiaux published in the journal *Applied Linguistics* in 1995 indicated that semicolon use has become increasingly infrequent since the nineteenth century. Bruthiaux's sample texts from the eighteenth century revealed a ratio of semicolon use of 68.1 semicolons per 1,000 words, which dropped to 17.7 semicolons per 1,000 words by the nineteenth century, perhaps reflecting the increased speed of reading and writing and the ascendance of shorter sentences.

From about 2013 the semicolon gained a new symbolic meaning in the language of tattoos. As conversations about mental health and suicide prevention became more pressing, a group of people formed Project Semicolon on social media and began using the semicolon as a symbol of their struggle. A tattoo of a semicolon came to symbolize choosing not to end your sentence (a metaphor for life), proclaiming itself as a positive symbol for overcoming mental health problems and continuing to live.

Apostrophe

Since its inception the apostrophe has been a controversial piece of punctuation. In part this is because its usage has shifted over time and the rules of its use took a long time to be codified; it is still somewhat in flux today. This has made the apostrophe a nebulous piece of our grammatical furniture, its confusing and ever-changing usage only serving to make it appear somewhat irrational and irksome. Perhaps the key to its elusive meaning is that it was not a mark which had roots in medieval manuscripts, like the full stop or colon. Instead it is thought the apostrophe was first introduced by French printer Geoffroy Tory in about 1529. Tory had successfully worked as a typographer and printer for a number of years; he was known especially for his style of decoration and for popularizing the use of roman type instead of the more prevalent Gothic type. In 1529 he published the philological work for which he is best known, *Champfleury*.

In this key text, Tory introduced a number of typographic symbols to improve the reading and understanding of written French. This included bringing in the cedilla (ç) from Spanish and adding an acute accent to *e* (é) to clarify pronunciation, plus the introduction of the apostrophe. Tory used the apostrophe to signify where letters were missing, in order to hark back to their Latin root.

This innovation and the numerous rules and clarifications on language Tory elucidated in *Champfleury* were extremely influential and soon spread to Britain. Printers began to use Tory's apostrophe to indicate not only where letters were missing from the Latin spellings but also where English letters were missing. Spelling was starting to become more regularized at this time and many old vowel usages were disappearing. For example, the word 'books' used to be spelt *bookes* or even *bookis* and so by the seventeenth century British printers were using *book's* to indicate where the vowel once appeared. Initially, then, the apostrophe's main role was to show what was missing.

By the end of the seventeenth century Britain had become increasingly literate, with one of the highest literacy rates in Europe. As a result many writers and printers were keen to further codify the written language, creating many rules and regulations, some of which remain to this day. It was at this point that the apostrophe also began to be used to show possession, in a nod to the eliding apostrophe's role in indicating missing vowels. The problem came when trying to codify the rules for apostrophes and plurals; no one, it seemed, could agree. Should the apostrophe come before or after the *s*? And what if the word itself is singular but ends with an *s*, such as news?

Due to the complexities of these questions and the numerous competing theories, the exact rules of apostrophe use have remained obscure for the majority of the population up to the present day. It does not help that their usage is still changing. Many place names and street signs now do away with an apostrophe, with King's Street now frequently rendered as Kings Street, and many high-street shops doing away with their possessive apostrophes too, such as Boots and Waterstones. However, this deflation in apostrophe use has been somewhat counteracted by the growth of the greengrocer's apostrophe. This incorrect usage is so-called due to the habit of fruit sellers (and other retailers) of wrongly inserting an apostrophe on the plural of a noun – for example, writing '10 apple's for £1' instead of '10 apples for £1'. Such is the frequency of this error that in future it may even become an accepted usage. In addition, people rarely now use apostrophes to show the traditional abbreviations of telephone ('phone) or aeroplane ('plane), and apostrophes cannot be used in a website address (URL), further weakening their grip in the modern world. Despite this, there are aspects of our multicultural globalized world which have increased apostrophe usage, such as romanized Arabic. Written words such as Qur'an (which in written Arabic uses a symbol known as hamza to indicate the glottal stop) are rendered with an apostrophe to help English speakers pronounce the words correctly.

In 2017 news reports revealed that a 'grammar vigilante' had been secretly at work in the Bristol area for over thirteen years. In the dead of night, armed only with a broom handle, some stickers and a sponge, the vigilante has been correcting misplaced apostrophes on local shop signs, indicating that for some the misuse of an apostrophe continues to rile.

Question mark

The question mark is today a useful piece of punctuation which makes an interrogative sentence easier to understand but also allows anyone reading aloud to inflect their voice upwards at the end to verbally signal the question.

There are two proposed roots for the distinctive shape of the question mark but neither is fully backed up by the textual record, leaving its exact origin obscure. It is worth outlining them here to give a fuller picture of the options discussed by scholars of punctuation. The first proposed origin is from Ancient Egypt, where they chose to use the shape of an inquisitive cat's tail as a symbol, potentially inspiring future grammarians to adopt this distinctive shape for the question mark. The second option derives from Latin and supposes that scribes would use a shortened version of *quaestio* (meaning 'question') at the end of a sentence to indicate that it was a question. Over time this was shortened to *qo*, and then the *qo* got further shortened, until the *q* was written over the *o*, later morphing into the now familiar question mark.

While we might not know the exact origin of the question mark, what we do know is that it was Alcuin of York (*c.*735–804) who popularized its use. Alcuin was a renowned English scholar and deacon of York. In 781 he met king of the Franks and future Holy Roman Emperor, Charlemagne (742–814), at Parma. Struck by Alcuin's intelligence and insight, Charlemagne invited him to move to his court at Aachen. There he worked on improving the church liturgy and promoting the Latin language. He became one of the leading scholars of the Carolingian Renaissance.

To improve the clarity of the reading experience Alcuin introduced the *punctus interrogativus*, or 'point of interrogation', which served as a modern question mark does at the end of a sentence. The mark was made with a tilde (~) or a vertical tilde resembling a flash of lightning over the top of a full stop. The great influence of Alcuin meant his works were widely circulated across Europe, and so his use of the *punctus interrogativus* soon spread, gradually developing into the sign we recognize today.

An earlier version of the question mark was proposed in 2011 by Cambridge University manuscript specialist Dr Chip Coakley. While studying versions of the Bible from the fifth century in the ancient Middle Eastern language Syriac, Coakley noticed that frequently two dots, rather like a colon, were employed above a word at the start of a sentence to indicate a question. The double dot is known as *zagwa elaya* by scholars of Syriac. It was Dr Coakley who first noted its use as signifier of a question, making it the earliest known usage in any language of a form of question mark. It seems likely that this symbol developed independently of the question mark developed by Alcuin.

In English the syntax of a question differs from a statement; for example, 'You are going to the beach' and 'Are you going to the beach?' In contrast in Spanish there is no change in sentence structure; so 'Vas a la playa' means 'You are going to the beach', whereas '¿Vas a la playa?' means: 'Are you going to the beach?' This means that in the Spanish language question marks need to be employed at both ends of a sentence to clearly indicate it is a question. In 1754 the Spanish Royal Academy decreed that the opening question mark (*signo de apertura de interrogación*) must be used at the start of all questions. In consequence this became the norm in written Spanish. Incidentally the smartphone (enemy of punctuation fans and grammarians everywhere) has begun to impact on the use of the opening question mark in Spanish. The opening question mark has become just another symbol to type, and in the age of speed and contraction it is an early casualty. It remains to be seen if this change will seep into formal written Spanish.

The question mark is not only used to indicate a question; it is also inserted into text to indicate a query. For example, if we are unclear of a date of death we might put: 'd. 1357?' Furthermore if we want to indicate that there is debate or confusion over the location of an event we might write: 'Birmingham (?)'. Additionally in modern casual usage people have come to use a series of question marks to add emphasis, expressing incredulity or horror, for example: 'What's for dinner? Liver and onions???'

Exclamation mark

The exclamation mark is a later addition to the canon of punctuation marks, seemingly first arriving fully formed in humanist printed texts in the fifteenth century. Unlike the practical, sensible comma and full stop, the exclamation mark is all show and verve – its very appearance drawing the eye and bringing emphasis to the text. The origin of the eye-catching mark is unclear, but the most commonly repeated story of its creation is notably one that links form and meaning. The story goes that the exclamation mark developed from the habit monastic scribes had of exclaiming joy in their devotional texts. In Latin the word for joy is *io*, which was written with a capital *I* above an *O*. It is said this shorthand for joy slowly morphed into the 'point of admiration', used in early printed texts to signify wonderment, a usage which continued until the 1700s. Alternatively, M.B. Parkes in *Pause and Effect* (1992) suggests that Italian poet Iacopo

Alpoleio da Urbisaglia claimed to have invented the *punctus admirativus* (as he called it) at the end of the fourteenth century, using a *punctus* (full stop) with a slanted dash above it to signify an exclamation. This rendering of the mark is also seen in some later humanist texts, such as Coluccio Salutati's Paris copy of *De nobilitate legum et medicinae* (1399) and likely seeped into more common usage from there.

In the eighteenth century writer and lexicographer Dr Samuel Johnson began to refer to this symbol as the exclamation mark, elaborating that it should be used to exclaim passions. In this way the mark shifted from revealing devotional wonder and admiration to a mark of emphasis.

The exclamation mark (or point in America) came into its own in novels and plays, helping the reader to decode the emphasis intended. It is used to convey the force of an involuntary ejaculation, 'Yikes!'; to add drama to a revelation, 'That's not a stranger; that's my mother!'; to indicate humour or disagreement, 'The children's park had a sign which read "keep off the grass"!'; to show admiration, 'What a beautiful house!'; to indicate shouting, 'Look out!'; and, its most common modern usage, to add emphasis, 'I am so excited!' Comic books have been especially fertile ground for the exclamation mark, its appearance adding brio to a fight scene with a Wham! Bam! Smash!

In an analysis of exclamation mark usage in the novels of selected writers for his book *Nabokov's Favorite Word is Mauve* (2017), Ben Blatt reveals that Elmore Leonard, contrary to his assertion that writers should only use an exclamation mark two or three times for every 100,000 words, in fact used it an average of forty-nine times per 100,000 words across forty-five novels. Proving that the exclamation mark has a long literary pedigree, Blatt reveals that in Jane Austen's six novels she utilizes the exclamation mark at a rate of 449 per 100,000 words. Top of Blatt's analysis, however, was James Joyce, who in the space of just three novels manages to use the exclamation mark 1,105 times per 100,000 words (!).

Traditionally the exclamation mark has been used sparingly, especially in formal writing. In some journalistic circles students were told they had one exclamation mark to use in their entire career, so to choose carefully when they would deploy it. Indeed, in H.W. Fowler's *A Dictionary of Modern English Usage* (1926) he cautions: 'Except in poetry the exclamation mark should be used sparingly.

Excessive use of exclamation marks in expository prose is a sure sign of an unpractised writer or of one who wants to add a spurious dash of sensation to something unsensational.' This sense of it as an exceptional mark to be deployed rarely is seemingly confirmed by the fact that before the 1970s it only infrequently appeared on typewriter keyboards and so had to be inserted by typing a full stop and then going back and typing an apostrophe above.

In recent times, however, digital communication has produced an exclamation mark inflation. Where once just a single exclamation mark would suffice to indicate the urgency of an email marked 'Important!' now we might more frequently use two, or even three!!! This inflation can in part be ascribed to the difficulty in conveying tone and emphasis online. The expression of excitement and admiration have especially benefited from the deployment of multiple exclamation marks, so much so that a single one now almost implies very little excitement at all, whereas deploying three shows you really are excited.

In modern online usage, then, the exclamation mark has evolved once again, away from intensity and towards warmth. The exclamation marks that litter our emails and text messages are now most often used to impart a tone of friendliness, adding some personality to an otherwise deadpan exchange. It is interesting to note that a number of studies (for example, a 2006 article by Carol Waseleski in the *Journal of Computer-Mediated Communication*) have found that women tend to use exclamation marks in digital communication more than men, arguing that, rather than showing 'excitability' as had previously (somewhat patronisingly) been suggested, they are in fact most commonly used to show cordiality. The increasing use of the exclamation mark in the digital age is another example of our ever-evolving relationship with punctuation. Writing and communication are not static, but are constantly growing and changing as methods of communication develop.

Ellipsis

The ellipsis (…) is an interesting piece of punctuation, indicating not the presence of something but rather an absence or a pause. Its use conveys the natural gaps in conversational speech, or the intriguing tailing off of a sentence. The word 'ellipsis' itself derives from the Greek *élleipsis*, which means to leave out or fall short. Its use was first seen in the English language in a grammatical context in the 1610s. Using an ellipsis in text to indicate speech or thought suddenly breaking off is called *aposiopesis* (from the Greek, 'becoming silent'). It has its roots in Ancient Greek rhetoric, which at the time did not have a textual mark; rather, it was a concept or device used in speech. Ellipsis as a sign of omission has been rendered in numerous ways over the years, with dots, dashes, asterisks or hyphens.

The first appearance of three dots on a page was on handwritten manuscripts from the fourteenth century; however, they did not represent the modern meaning of an ellipsis. Instead these medieval dots were known as subpuncting or underdotting and were used by scribes to indicate where a word had been erroneously copied and should therefore be scrubbed out. Subpuncting continued until the early sixteenth century and then, as the printing press changed how books were produced, its usage in this context died out. It is not clear whether the textual use of three dots in subpuncting was a precursor to the modern ellipsis, but it seems possible that this existing mark was adopted and adapted by early typographers.

In early printed works, periods of silence were marked textually with a series of hyphens. Dr Anne Toner of Cambridge University, who has spent years researching the ellipsis, uncovered what she thinks is its first use, in an English translation of Roman dramatist Terence's play *Andria*, printed in 1588. Although the play uses hyphens instead of dots, the general idea appeared to catch on rapidly – Toner notes that although there are only four 'ellipses' in the 1588 translation, there are 29 in the 1627 version. By the eighteenth century, dots started to replace the dashes, and as their use in printed works grew three dots became the standardized form of conveying an ellipsis, whereas a dash might signal an interruption.

Typographically and stylistically, even today no consensus exists on the exact rendering of the ellipsis. Some say three dots in a row, no spaces. Others prefer three dots each separated by a space. A third way is to use a keyboard shortcut to type it as a single-character glyph – a device that means it cannot run over the end of a line. People today might say 'dot dot dot' at the end of a sentence to signify that they are leaving things unsaid, in a sort of verbal cliffhanger. For example, 'Strange, it was the Christmas party last night and today Valerie is not in work dot, dot, dot.' Virginia Woolf was the first writer to use a spoken ellipsis in the form of a character saying 'dot dot dot' in her short story 'An Unwritten Novel' (1920).

Recently the ellipsis has grown in importance in digital communication. A full stop is final – as if shutting down debate – whereas the trailing off offered by an ellipsis opens up room for reply and demonstrates uncertainty and the potential for debate. For example, there is a certain finality to 'I am going to vote for the Monster Raving Loony Party'; whereas 'I am going to vote for the Monster Raving Loony Party…' implies the speaker's mind isn't quite made up and they are open to discussion. In the age of social media, where engagement with followers is key, the ellipsis as an invitation to open conversation has come into its own.

Quotation marks

Quoted text was first distinguished by monks in Byzantium in the sixth century. These Greek texts would show passages quoted from the Bible, and therefore God's words, by placing the multitasking *diple* (meaning 'double' > on account of the two marks used to write one) in the margin on each line of quoted text. This useful device soon spread from the Byzantine Empire to the Latin texts of the West. Western monks began to use the marginal *diple* not just for God's word but also to distinguish quotations from other devotional works, expanding its use. However, it was not a straightforward route from the *diple* to the double quotation mark. As with many other punctuation marks, the plethora of different scribal hands and the lack of any concerted rules on punctuation during this early period meant that soon the *diple* as a quotation mark was being rendered in a variety of different ways. This meant that no clear mark won out and for hundreds of years quotations were indicated in a variety of ways or not at all.

Even the introduction of the printing press, which was often the moment at which a particular mark was set, did not resolve the confusion. Typographer and historian Douglas Crawford McMurtrie suggested that the first instance of quotation marks in a printed book were found in 1516 in *De Vitis Sophistarum* by Flavius Philostratus, printed in Strasbourg by Mathias Schurer. These appear as what we would recognize as closing double quotations marks (that is, they are inverted) and appear in the margin at the start of each sentence of quoted text, raised to distinguish them from ordinary commas. However, this did not immediately become standard. In some early printed Bibles quoted text is indicated by changing the font from roman to italic or by simply naming the speaker. During the sixteenth century a rival mark was introduced in France: two chevron brackets « at the start of the quoted passage, with two chevrons facing the other way at the close ». Printer Guillaume Le Bé (1525–1598) has been credited with their adoption and the marks are named in his honour as *guillemets*. Despite them being named in his honour, Le Bé plainly was not the first to use them, as they are thought to have first appeared in a printed book in 1527, when he would have been just a baby. Guillemets, however, proved popular and remain the key method of indicating quotations in French, Arabic, Italian, Greek and many other languages.

Despite these bold advances in marking out quotations, a variety of methods were still employed, and in fact many texts still omitted any indication of cited material at all. In the 1570s the use of the *diple* (or commas or brackets) to indicate quoted text was expanded to include marking passages of direct speech. This was a useful aid to the reader. However, it was not until the eighteenth century, when the novel came into its own, and with it the need to distinguish direct speech more clearly from narration, that the need for a consistent symbol became apparent. Initially printers used a number of different methods, from paragraph breaks to dashes, but as the eighteenth century wore on it became increasingly common in English novels to see the use of opening and closing quotation marks, their previous position in the margin eschewed for inclusion in the main body of the text. These literary quotation marks developed as a visual aid to the reader, indicating a change in voice, unlike earlier marks such as full stops and commas, which were originally created to enable the text to be read aloud with the correct pauses.

The novel had ushered in greater consistency in the use of opening and closing quotation marks, but confusion still reigned on the issue of double or single marks, which were often used interchangeably. By the nineteenth century lines in the sand were being drawn, with the Americans opting for double quotation marks, while the English favoured single – a state of play that largely continues to this day. Quotation marks (in both their single and double form) are also often used to indicate foreign words or the titles of books, plays or songs – although these days italicizing is conventional for published works. A physical sign of the quotation mark has also sprung up, with people using two fingers to curl up and down in 'air quotes' to show an audience when they are quoting someone, or more often than not to indicate the ironic effect of another's words. In written text this same device is called 'scare quotes' – quotation marks used to indicate that the word thus enclosed is not one the writer of the text would use and confers a certain amount of disdain. For example: 'teenagers like to refer to their fancy new trainers as "fresh creps".'

Curly quotation marks almost saw their end in the 1860s when early typewriter manufacturers began selecting the symbols to add to their keyboards. It was deemed far more efficient to use a key with a single raised straight short dash ' which could be used as an apostrophe, as single quotation marks, or typed twice as double, at both the start and the end of a quotation. This thinking persisted into the development of the coding of symbols to be used online; the straight quotation mark is widely used across the Internet, while curly marks still adorn printed works such as books and newspapers.

Brackets

I am a big fan of brackets (they allow me to add asides) and I use them liberally. Brackets almost always come in pairs (an exception being when they are used as part of an emoticon ;) – see page 101) and are used to enclose a word or sentence that reveals extra information about the topic in question. The bracket did not appear in early or medieval writings; it is early modern in origin, first appearing in late-fourteenth- and early-fifteenth-century texts. Unlike many early punctuation marks which arose from the reading of texts aloud, the bracket was clearly created for those who read silently. The information within the brackets is almost like a stage direction to the reader or an aside, and would not necessarily be spoken aloud.

The word 'parenthesis' originally comes from a Greek root, meaning roughly 'a putting in beside', a meaning which sums up its purpose. The first written parentheses were within chevron brackets

< > and appear in Coluccio Salutati's *De nobilitate legum et medicinae* of 1399. Further early examples appear in works copied by Florentine humanists in the 1420s. The chevron brackets were soon largely superseded by the curved brackets we use today, after Gasparino Barzizza (*c.* 1359–1431) recommended their use in his treatise on punctuation *Doctrina punctandi*. As if confirming their utility, early designers of fonts, such as Aldus Manutius, included brackets, ensuring the innovation was spread around Europe, arriving in England in 1494. In 1531 Erasmus wrote of brackets, calling them *lunula*, as their crescent shape recalls the form of the moon.

Brackets come in four forms; initially all were interchangeable but over time each type has come to be used in a specific context. Curved brackets () are used most commonly in writing to provide extra information or an afterthought. Curly brackets {}, or braces, are today predominantly used in mathematical contexts or in computer programming languages such as Java, to group together related numbers or at the start or end of a particular command. Square brackets [], also known as crotchets, are often used in traditional text to fill in information where gaps have been left in a testimony or as an aside from the editor. For example, a defendant might respond to questioning: 'It wasn't me; it was him [pointing to his brother]'. Or when quoting someone who uses a word incorrectly one might insert the Latin word *sic* (Latin 'thus', meaning 'spelled as given') in square brackets to indicate the mistake is in the source; for example, 'She said the event was "a damp squid [*sic*]" (she meant, of course, "damp squib").' The final type of bracket is also the oldest: the chevron bracket <> , which today is widely used in Standard Generalized Markup Language (SGML), HTML and coding. In this context the chevron brackets contain the unseen instructions to the computer on how a page or table should be laid out on-screen.

A further modern use of the beautiful curved line of the bracket is to demonstrate a hug online. You might visually show your support for someone by enclosing their name thus: (((Charlotte))). This rather lovely use of the bracket was subverted and then reappropriated by Twitter users in 2016. Far-right trolls began using three brackets either side of someone's name (known as echoes) as a secret signal to their followers that the person thus enclosed was Jewish. Most Twitter users were naturally disgusted by this anti-Semitic labelling. Many decided to show solidarity and reclaim the triple bracket by applying it to their own Twitter handles, thereby making the alt-right use of the brackets null and void.

Hyphen

As the proud owner of my very own hyphen in a lovingly crafted surname, I have an especial soft spot for this most confusing of punctuation marks. To illustrate its importance we have the tale of the 'most expensive hyphen in history' (according to Arthur C. Clarke). In 1962 NASA was launching an interplanetary probe, *Mariner 1*, with the mission to fly by Venus. Unfortunately a crucial hyphen was omitted from the coding which specified its speed and trajectory, causing it to explode on take-off. This tragic story is really more telling about the importance of accuracy in coding than hyphen usage, but I like the fact that it all hinges on a hyphen. Perhaps what is more illustrative of the importance (or otherwise) of the hyphen is that as I wrote that sentence I realized that I should consult the indispensable *New Oxford Dictionary for Writers and Editors* to check whether as a noun 'take off' is written as 'takeoff', 'take off' or 'take-off' (it advises the last). That hyphenation remains an issue of contention, with competing style guides promoting differing uses, is what makes the hyphen so hard to pin down.

The origin of the hyphen (or, more specifically, a 'soft hyphen', one that links words in printed text which are broken by a line break) can be traced to father of the printing press Johannes Gutenberg himself. When printing the first books, Gutenberg was keen that his newly automated machine would create pages that looked as close as possible to those produced by scribes. Traditionally, handwritten works were laid out fully justified, with the monks varying the word spacing or size of script to ensure the blocks of text remained flush with neat margins. In order to replicate this look, Gutenberg assidu-ously introduced a hyphen to link words that were forcibly broken by pushing them onto the next line of text to keep the work justified. So enthusiasti-cally did Gutenberg employ the hyphen that he even used it in ways that would shock any modern typographer, such as not sticking to syllables as places to break, and even creating a single letter break! Gutenberg's soft hyphen continues to be used by typographers, albeit with more sensible rules and regulations for its deployment, for text that needs to be justified. Thankfully, since the creation of modern word-processing software, the computer can take care of justification by increasing or decreasing the space between words, taking tricky decisions on soft hyphen usage out of our hands (although typographers still need to struggle with these decisions).

The hard hyphen, however, is still a knotty problem. The hard hyphen is used to make one word out of two words and is one of those additions to written English language which keeps writers reaching for their style guide of choice. The loss of 16,000 hyphens from words in the sixth edition of the *Shorter Oxford English Dictionary* in 2007 sparked a flurry of concerned headlines. Particularly puzzling was that not all the removed hyphens created closed-up words. For example, the hyphen was removed from 'fig leaf', 'pot belly' and 'test tube', leaving two words in its place. However, the hyphen was also removed from 'bumblebee', 'chickpea' and 'leapfrog', leaving a single word. The justification was that this shorter version of the *OED* was designed to reflect common usage and therefore did not necessarily follow hard-and-fast rules. Therein lies the problem. There is no consensus for hyphenating compound nouns and so each dictionary or style guide tends to set its own standards, with some opting for plentiful hyphenation and others opting for a light touch. The hyphen should be used to clarify meaning. This can be demonstrated by the use of the hyphen in a compound adjective; after all, there is quite a difference in meaning between 'thirty odd men' and 'thirty-odd men'.

Although hyphens may be slowly fading from modern writing, especially with the informality of email (or should that be e-mail?), they are enjoying a resurgence in linking together surnames. Today with women less keen to surrender their names on marriage and with the increase in same-sex marriages, single surnames are increasingly being usurped by hyphenated names. Traditionally the female name came first, but today (as in my surname) any which way goes, and people more often than not choose the order that sounds the best (or, again in my case, the least worst).

Glyphs

We are symbols, and inhabit symbols.
Ralph Waldo Emerson, 'The Poet', 1844

Whereas, strictly speaking, all the symbols in this book can be described as glyphs, I am choosing to use the word to group together those useful symbols which are neither punctuation nor mathematical symbols. The glyphs included here really are the special characters of the keyboard. They are the symbols whose form immediately encapsulates a meaning (even if that meaning has changed over time) in a way that punctuation cannot. Where punctuation clarifies the written word, its deployment changing or emphasizing the meaning of a sentence, a glyph usually indicates one clear message. For example, by using the dollar sign you are indicating that the number quoted after it represents an amount of money in American dollars.

Rather than being part of the structure of a sentence, a glyph represents a meaning which when placed next to another word or number serves to supply context. For example, the copyright symbol next to a person's name immediately tells us that the artwork/song/piece of writing belongs to that individual, thereby communicating a whole concept with the addition of just one tiny character.

Perhaps because we don't get to use glyphs as often as we use standard punctuation it feels a bit more special to roll one out. Their form is somehow more substantial than a piece of punctuation, often entailing a number of pen strokes. They do not have the subjective or style-driven rules that make navigating punctuation often fraught territory. You know where you are with a pound sign.

The symbols in this section were mostly born of an abbreviation; for example, the ampersand is a shortened version of *et* ('and' in Latin). However, this does not mean that their meaning is unchangeable. A couple of the glyphs featured in this section, @ and #, started out life meaning one thing, and then, thanks to their use by early-adopter computer programmers and developers, they came to have a whole new meaning.

Of all the pictograms and glyphs created, only a few have persisted through to the modern day and find a space on keyboards (and inclusion in this book). Their continued use was perhaps ensured by their clear and simple meaning (£, $ and €), by their beautiful form (&, *) or through their modern reinvention (@ and #). The glyphs included in this section do not have an overarching theme linking them together in the same way that punctuation or mathematical symbols do. Instead, what joins them is their ability to communicate their meaning visually.

Hash sign

The hashtag, hash or pound sign, as it's traditionally known in the USA, has its origins in the shorthand used by medieval scribes for the Latin *libra pondo*, which translates as 'pound by weight'. They used the abbreviation *lb*, but this was sometimes misread as *16*. As a consequence, by the fourteenth century scribes took to drawing a line through the top of the two letters – or, as some sources suggest, not a line but a tilde (see page 162) – to indicate that the word was itself an abbreviation. This in time developed into the now familiar #.

The symbol is also sometimes used to denote a number, as in #4. As a result, in some contexts it is known as the number sign. In chess notation the # denotes checkmate, in proofreading it means 'insert a space' and in computer programming it indicates that the rest of the line of script after the # is for comment only and not part of the program. The word 'hash' came into common usage in the 1910s to denote the stripes on a military uniform; by the 1980s 'hash' had come to be associated with the # sign, but the sign itself had no accepted usage and was used infrequently.

The hash sign's journey into ubiquity began in the 1960s, when it was selected by Bell Laboratories to be a function key on their newly designed touch-tone telephone keypad. At that time the hash sign served no real function and yet was familiar because it was arbitrarily included on most standard type-writers. The Bell Labs team fondly nicknamed the symbol the 'octothorpe' – 'octo' because the symbol has eight tips. The reasons behind the 'thorpe' are more obscure, however. Some suggest this part of the word was named in honour of American athlete Jim Thorpe (of whom the team at Bell Labs were big fans), but other sources trace its etymology to the Old Norse meaning of *thorpe*, 'farmstead' or 'field', which would make the portmanteau octothorpe 'eight fields', effectively describing the hash sign's physical shape.

Although, thanks to Bell Laboratories, the # had become ubiquitous on telephone and computer keypads, it did not really have a firm use, varying from denoting weight to signifying numbers or simply as a button to press when communicating with an automated system through your telephone. However, all this changed in 2007, when early Twitter users began discussing methods to filter and group the messages on their feeds. Developer Chris Messina proposed that Twitter adopt the method previously used in IRC (Internet Relay Chat), an early form of social media, whereby users used the # to flag up the subject of their conversation. This became known as a 'hashtag' as the hash sign was now being used to 'tag' content. This innovation allowed users to search by hashtag and therefore isolate the posts that related to their interests. It was an organic development, as Katie Jacobs Stanton of Twitter explains: 'Twitter didn't make up the hashtag. Twitter didn't make up the retweet. It's our users. And people started using them so much that we decided to weave them into the product.' The method was so simple that it quickly caught on, first on Twitter and soon across all social media, gifting the hash sign with a renewed lease of life.

Today it is suggested that Twitter users alone use some 125 million hashtags every day, which is an incredible ascendancy for the humble hash sign. Hashtags are not just for inane postings on Facebook (#makingmemories) but have recently become more visible and vital as online activism (or 'hashtag activism', as coined by the *Guardian* in 2011) has grown. The development of the #BlackLivesMatter and #MeToo movements (among many others) have demonstrated how messages can spread and voices can be magnified by the umbrella of a strong hashtag. By dint of the measurement of popularity of hashtags in the 'trending' listing on Twitter, people can now circumvent traditional media and get issues pushed to the top of an agenda by wisely using or creating a powerful hashtag, raising voices which might not otherwise get heard.

At sign

Historians and lexicographers have searched for the origin of the @ in medieval manuscripts but no trace of it has been found. Despite this absence of evidence a number of theories as to its creation are put forward which link it to scribal hands. Some propose that the @ was first used by tired scribes who were fed up with the long hours of copying and so invented a number of abbreviations to lighten the load. These weary scribes supposedly shortened the Latin *ad* (meaning 'at' or 'towards') by curling the tail of the *d* to wrap it around the *a*, thereby saving themselves two whole pen strokes. Another hypothesis is that it derives from the French *à* (also meaning 'at') whereby the accent was incorporated into the glyph, but again this scribal shortcut doesn't really make sense for an already short word.

Based on physical evidence, the @ sign seems to have a mercantile origin. The first use of the sign has been ascribed to a letter by Florentine merchant Francesco Lapi in 1536. Lapi used the @ as a shortening of *amphorae* – a unit of measurement for the wine, grains and spices that were shipped in the large clay jars of the same name. It went on to be used by other merchants to denote 'at the rate of', written out as '15 apples @ 15p each'. As a result, it became known in English as the 'commercial at'. This origin of the symbol makes sense in English, but when one reflects that in numerous other languages the name of the symbol relates to a variety of animals – for example, in Dutch 'monkey's tail'; in Danish 'elephant's trunk'; in Norwegian 'pig's tail' – the question arises as to whether we have truly got to the bottom of this strange symbol's creation.

The modern and now ubiquitous use of the @ in email addresses and Twitter handles has a more traceable history. In 1971 computer scientist Ray Tomlinson was working for BBN Technologies in Cambridge, Massachusetts, as they worked to create the forerunner of the Internet, the Arpanet. Tomlinson was pondering the difficult question of how to connect computer programmers to one another so that they might exchange messages. He decided that each person should have an address made up of their name joined to an as-yet-undecided symbol, followed by the name of their computer

– this would enable computers to read and understand the address and ensure it reached the right person. Tomlinson searched the keyboard for an underused symbol and alighted on the @. Using the @ to join name and computer, Tomlinson wrote the first email and sent it through the Arpanet – the @ sign was given a new purpose in life.

As online communication has developed, the @ has become the standard way of addressing an email, joining the user name to the mail server. In this way it has become linked to an address or destination, and so is now also used in front of a person's username or handle on Instagram or Twitter (for example, you can find me @nonfictioness). Likewise, it is often used online as an abbreviation: 'c u @ the pub'. With the advent of online trolling, people have now taken to writing sometimes controversial opinions on social media and then adding the caveat 'Don't @ me' to try to prevent other users from replying directly, the implication being that they don't care what you think of their opinion (which, while a nice idea, rarely has the desired effect). Thanks to the omnipresent language of the Internet the @ is now at home on computer keyboards all over the world. The symbol's name may differ but its meaning is now universal.

Ampersand

One of the earliest examples of the written ampersand was preserved in graffiti on a wall in Pompeii by the eruption of Vesuvius in 79 CE. The logogram (a character used to represent a word or phrase) was created as a ligature for shortening the Latin *et* (meaning 'and'), allowing the word to be written in one flowing stroke of the pen. The symbol and its meaning spread with the Roman Empire. Many scribes interpreted their own form for the handy ligature, adding flourishes and changes which make many early ampersands very different from the modern recognized form. By 775 CE the ampersand (although it was not then known as this) was officially added to the Roman alphabet and as a result was also later tacked onto the English alphabet as if it were the twenty-seventh letter.

With the introduction of printing in the mid-fifteenth century, type cutters adapted this handy ligature from the written to the printed page. A number of different styles were cut; some early typefaces used an ampersand closer to the original *e* and *t* of *et* than we see standardized today. The many shapes of the ampersand have long fascinated typographers. One of the most thorough investigations into the typographic history of the ampersand was carried out by German graphic designer Jan Tschichold. In 1953 he published *A Brief History of the Ampersand* as a sort of love letter to the ampersand, in which he collected many examples, from the first century onwards, visually charting its developing form.

The ampersand, although widely used, did not 'officially' have a name until the nineteenth century. From the 1700s, when British schoolchildren would recite letters aloud for dictation they were instructed to use the Latin *per se* (to mean 'by itself') before any single letter such as *i* or *a*. For example, when spelling out a sentence beginning 'I wish…' the children would chant '*i per se, w, i, s, h…*' so that the listener would understand that the first *i* stood alone and was not attached to the following word. This meant that, in reciting their alphabet, when the children got to the end, in order to incorporate the twenty-seventh 'letter' they would finish with '*x, y, z* and *per se and*', indicating that the *&* stood on its own. Over time the speed at which the children chanted their alphabet caused the final section to blend into one word, 'ampersand', and the word for the previously unnamed symbol was coined, entering the dictionary in 1837.

Today the ampersand is frequently seen in branding and advertising – H&M, M&S, Barnes & Noble – its beautiful curvy lines lending itself well to logos, but it is rarely seen in other contexts. Some style guides allow an ampersand to clarify a list (although a semicolon or Oxford comma is more commonly used for this function). For example, 'My favourite foods are pizza, pasta, fish & chips and sausages'. Another obscure official usage of the ampersand is laid out by the Writers Guild of America, which specifies that an ampersand between two writers' names denotes that they collaborated on a project, whereas using 'and' between their names shows they both worked on the script (perhaps one correcting or improving the other's work) but not at the same time.

Despite its declining use in long-form writing the ampersand's prominent position on modern computer keyboards is likely to be retained. Since the twentieth century it has formed a key part of many computer programming languages, such as

C++; however, exactly what the *&* means in each programming language differs. The ampersand may no longer have the cachet of being the twenty-seventh letter of the alphabet, but its back-room job for computer programmers ensures it is still a vital and well-used glyph.

Asterisk

Sumerian pictographic writing includes a sign for 'star' which looks like a modern asterisk. These early writings from 5,000 years ago are the first known depiction of an asterisk; however, it seems unlikely that these pictograms are the forerunner of the symbol we use today. Palaeographers know that Aristarchus of Samothrace (220–143 BCE) used an asterisk symbol when editing Homer in the second century BCE, because later scholars wrote about him doing so. Physical examples of Aristarchus' asterisks have not survived so we cannot know their physical shape, but as the word 'asterisk' derives from the Greek *asteriskos*, meaning 'little star', an assumption has been made that they resembled a small star. Aristarchus used the symbols to mark places in Homer's text that he was copying where he thought passages were from another source. By the third century CE Origen of Alexandria had adopted the asterisk when compiling the Hexapla – a Greek translation of the Jewish scriptures, the Septuagint. Origen used the asterisk to demarcate texts that he had added to the Septuagint from the original Hebrew. Both these early uses of the asterisk are as an editing tool, to notify the reader that the passage they are reading should be read with caution.

In the medieval period the asterisk continued to be employed in the copying of Bibles to flag up text from other sources. It also was increasingly used as a *signe de renvoi* (sign of return) – a graphic symbol which indicates where a correction or insertion should be made, with a corresponding mark in the margin with the correct text inserted. The asterisk is also found in medieval texts as a sign of omission. The use of the asterisk by scribes copying the Bible continued with the advent of the printing press; early printed Bibles, such as Robert Estienne's 1532 Latin Bible, make use of an asterisk. Scribes did not always use the modern asterisk shape, some instead adopting a hooked cross with dots between each arm. However, when the asterisk was cut into type it was rendered as the five- or six-pointed star, and this is the form that has largely endured.

The asterisk (often used interchangeably with the dagger or obelus) persisted as an editing mark but was also frequently used as a caveat, showing that the passage highlighted by the asterisk was served by a footnote or side note. By the eighteenth century the asterisk was being deployed as a sort of censorship, covering up letters to represent a d**n vulgar word without actually b****y spelling it out. But, as W. Somerset Maugham points out, this has become somewhat outmoded: 'We have long passed the Victorian Era when asterisks were followed after a certain interval by a baby.' A similar method, however, is still employed in comics, where it is known as grawlix, although the swear words are usually represented by a series of graphical glyphs, for example %@~#$!, rather than just asterisks. One of the problems with using asterisks to deaden the effect of a swear word is that it just draws attention to it (sometimes simply because one spends ages trying to work out which word the author is censoring).

In modern printed books the asterisk is most likely to show up as a method to mark footnotes. In advertising and on packaging it is generally a caveat – an advert might state 'Free Beer*' but when you follow the asterisk you discover in the terms and conditions that to claim the free beer you must sign over your firstborn. Online and on instant messaging, asterisks have become increasingly useful and now provide a series of services; for example, to show emphasis, in the way italics are used on the printed page. This use probably started on certain online forums where to make a word show up as bold it needed to be surrounded by asterisks, like *this*. This convention then crept online where, rather than using bold to show emphasis, the asterisks serve the purpose instead.

It is also frequently used for corrections when you male a spelling mistake.

*make

The asterisk is also used online as a way to give stage directions, such as *clears throat*, a use which *adopts exasperated expression* can be annoying.

Slash

The slash could just as easily find its place in the punctuation or the mathematical symbol section, because in its long history it has functioned as both. However, I have decided to classify it here as a glyph, simply because it has morphed from a piece of punctuation into a more utilitarian symbol, which I think better fits into the glyph category.

This symbol has only been known as the 'slash' since the 1960s; before that it was more commonly known as the virgule, solidus, oblique or stroke. As the virgule the symbol was commonly deployed as punctuation by medieval scribes, utilizing the handy symbol for any number of purposes – as a comma, a paragraph break or a colon. The virgule was quick and easy to write, its size meaning it did not get lost in the text. In the 1470s British printer William Caxton began using the virgule solely as a comma in the books he printed and it began to look like this would be the virgule's long-time role. That is, until printer extraordinaire Aldus Manutius came along and invented the comma (see page 17) in the 1490s. A hangover of this symbol interchange can be found in the French language, where a comma is known as a *virgule* despite no longer being represented by a virgule symbol itself. With the comma function now sewn up by the comma symbol, the virgule looked set to fade into obscurity.

Fortunately the virgule found a new niche – as a symbol to represent the word 'or', as in 'she/he', 'yes/no' or 'and', as in 'my cousin is an influencer/artist/student'. This use of the virgule as a separator continues; for example, it is deployed when quoting poetry running on in the text, the slashes representing line breaks. It is also used in the writing out of a date in figures: for example, 25/12/2007 (in the USA 12/25/2007). Similarly it can be used to show an abbreviation, such as 'a/c' to mean 'air conditioning'. In all these contexts, when reading aloud today we tend to call the virgule a slash, a development which began in relation to printing in the 1960s. It is unclear why it was so renamed at that time, but the pleasingly onomatopoeic name seems to fit in well with its new role as a separator.

Today the slash is also frequently used in Internet addresses in what is known as 'slash notation'.

In very basic terms, a forward slash is used to show a subsection of a main website. For example, bbc.co.uk/weather would take you to the weather pages of the BBC website, and bbc.co.uk/weather/ guildford would take you to the BBC weather pages on Guildford. Computer programmers term it the 'forward slash' to differentiate it from the 'backslash' – the symbol slanting the other way, which was introduced in 1961 for the sole use of programmers. This makes sense for programmers because they are familiar with the backslash, but for the rest of us who have no need for a backslash it can remain, simply, a slash.

In numerical notation the slash has another name and role, which developed entirely separately from the virgule but is now served by the same symbol on our keyboards. The solidus is today another name for the slash that is used in mathematical contexts to separate fractions. It gains its name from the Roman gold coin the *solidus*. When in the sixteenth century mathematicians were beginning to develop symbols instead of writing out long equations in words, Italian merchants started to use the useful long *s* symbol of the solidus ∫ to place between fractions, as the figures placed one on top of the other were hard to read. This useful device soon caught on; the curls at either end of the symbol were eventually dropped, until it resembled the /. In Britain the Roman method of denoting money, *l*, *s* and *d* (for *libra*, *solidus* and *denari*), had long been used in print for British equivalents, so *l* represented a pound, *s* a shilling and *d* pennies. When the Italian solidus symbol arrived in Britain, it was soon adopted as a symbol for writing out the shilling, so two shillings and sixpence would be written out as 2/6.

Although the solidus and the virgule have different roots, today the slash fulfils both purposes and many more besides. It is a symbol of utility that can be deployed in any number of ways, its purposeful form providing a visual separator. Today it is also used verbally to show different options (those coming after the slash often being the more subversive/ favoured). For example, 'Shall we meet at the café slash pub?', 'Come over for some tea slash wine.' The slash is a great example of a simple but useful glyph which early on lost its original purpose but was soon successfully repurposed, showing that even symbols can be reused and recycled.

Pound sign

To understand the pound sign one must first understand the origin of the pound. The pound, or *libra pondo*, was a unit of weight used in Ancient Rome, and it is also from here that we gain the abbreviation *lb* to represent a pound in weight. The measurement gave its name to currency because in the Roman system of *libra*, *solidus* and *denarius* the libra was a pound of silver which was used to make the 240 denarii that formed its value. Likewise 12 silver denarii were the equivalent value of 1 gold solidus. This monetary system was later adapted and adopted by the Carolingians in the eighth century. King Offa of Mercia saw the utility of this system and in *c.* 790 CE introduced it into his kingdom as pennies, with 240 pennies made from one pound of silver (which came to be known as the 'Tower pound'). Offa's coins were of such high quality that they were widely copied across the Anglo-Saxon kingdoms and into Europe. By the thirteenth century the currency had become known as 'sterling', probably deriving from the Germanic root *ster*, meaning strong, as the English currency was renowned for its high quality. An alternate etymology is put forward by the *Oxford English Dictionary*, which suggests 'sterling' derives from the Old English *steorling*, applied to Norman coins embossed with a star (*steorra*). Soon large amounts of money were referred to as 'pounds of sterlings', which over time became simply 'pound sterling', the unit of currency we still use today.

In the eleventh century William the Conqueror added to the system by introducing shillings, of which there were 20 to the pound, although at this stage the pound was still a notional coin and referred to the weight rather than an actual physical gold coin. It is Henry VII (1457–1509) who is credited with introducing a heavy gold coin in 1489, now known as the Tudor sovereign, which finally provided a coin to the value of a pound. The sovereign could be used for very large transactions but was mostly a coin of prestige, demonstrating the might of the English Crown.

By the fifteenth century there was a coin to represent the pound; the currency was widely known as 'pound sterling' and yet no symbol existed to express it. The exact moment the symbol was developed has been lost but its roots can be traced to the Latin abbreviations widely used in government. Currency was generally referred to in documents using the Latin *libra*, *solidus* and *denarius*. This meant it was written out in short as *l* to represent a pound, *s* for shilling and *d* for pennies. This shorthand persisted in books and newspapers right up to the nineteenth century.

A rival symbol had been in use for some time; it derived from the same root but had a rather more fancy form. This is the pound sign we know and love today. The Bank of England Museum has a cheque from 1661 with a handwritten pound sterling sign created from an elaborate capital *L* with a line (other instances have two) through it to show it is an abbreviation (of *libra*). (This system of creating a currency symbol has persisted with the symbol for the Japanese yen, created from a *Y* with two lines through it. Likewise, American cents are shown by a *C* with a vertical line through it.) It is unclear when this version of the pound symbol was first designed, but this cheque is the first known instance of the pound sign in use, and we know that by 1694, when the Bank of England was formally established, the symbol was in regular use. The two symbols remained in tandem use for many years until the twentieth century when the more distinct £ symbol became a more popular choice than the *l*. In recent times the symbol has taken on a political edge after it was used as a logo by UKIP, the (anti-European) United Kingdom Independence Party. That the power of a glyph has been harnessed by a political party to represent British sovereignty demonstrates the ability of a symbol to encapsulate a concept, for good or ill.

Dollar sign

The dollar sign is one of the most iconic symbols on our computer keyboards and has become intrinsically tied to capitalism and its home, America. However, the source of the symbol is far from clear, with numerous theories competing for the origin of the famous sign. The situation is not helped by the fact that there are two acceptable versions of the symbol – an *S* with one line through it and an *S* with two lines through it. But before we look at the confusing roots of the symbol we need to first understand the origin of the dollar itself.

The dollar did not originate in America; its beginning was in the silver mines of Joachimsthal in Bohemia (today in the Czech Republic and known as Jáchymov). These coins were first minted in 1519 and known as *Joachimsthaler*, which became shortened to *thaler*. The *thaler* was used across Europe; the Dutch called it the *daler*. It was the early Dutch immigrants who first took the coin to the new colonies of America. At first, because there was a severe shortage of British currency, a number of foreign coins were legal tender in the American colonies – the Spanish peso and the Portuguese 8-real piece, both large silver coins of similar weight and quality, were used interchangeably. This ultimately led to all large silver coins being referred to as 'dollar', the English corruption of the Dutch *daler*. Hence, when the colonies gained their independence they adopted the more familiar dollar as their official currency, rather than keeping the British pound.

The origin of the word 'dollar' therefore preceded the establishment of the United States of America in 1776, which debunks one theory of the birth of the dollar sign. In 1957, in her novel *Atlas Shrugged*, Ayn Rand suggested that the symbol derived from the initials of the United States – the *U* and the *S* superimposed over one another, which over time caused the bend of the *U* to be deleted, leaving the now familiar symbol. This cannot be true, however, because until 1776 the United States was known as the United Colonies of America and the first written dollar signs were found in merchants' records from the 1770s, before the name change.

Another view is that the sign comes from the source of the silver used to mint the coins circulating in America. Spanish conquistadors conquered the Inca and Aztec Empires in Mexico and Peru and plundered their silver, creating a new mint in Potosi, from where Spanish traders took the coins all over the world, making them one of the most important contemporary currencies. These coins were minted in 1767–70 and stamped with *PTSI* (short for Potosi), the characters superimposed over each other, in a symbol which looks like an *S* entwining a *T*. Many numismatists read this symbol as an early dollar sign.

A similar theory, and the one that most historians subscribe to, is that the sign derived from the Spanish peso. When writing out the currency, merchants would write a large *P* with a superscript *s*, thus: P^s. This was later simplified with the pillar of the *P* superimposed over the *S* – creating a dollar sign. A further link to the Spanish peso comes from the Pillars of Hercules, which were stamped on Spanish coins in the eighteenth and nineteenth centuries. The Ancient Greeks used the phrase 'Pillar of Hercules' to describe the two promontories that flank the Straits of Gibraltar. A symbol to represent the promontories depicted two pillars with banners wrapped around them, forming an *S* shape. This symbol formed part of the Spanish coat of arms and was stamped upon Spanish coins. In 1492, when the pillars were adopted as a symbol by Ferdinand II of Aragon, he added the legend *non plus ultra* in Latin, meaning 'nothing further beyond', signifying that Spain was the tip of the known world. However, once Christopher Columbus had 'discovered' America the words were changed to *plus ultra* ('further beyond') to denote that there were indeed lands beyond the Straits of Gibraltar. It is possible that these symbols on the widely used Spanish peso formed the origin of the now familiar dollar sign.

Although the exact birth of the dollar symbol cannot be traced, we can see it starting to appear in the written record from the end of the eighteenth century. One such example is in the letters and ledgers of Oliver Pollock, an Irish trader based in New Orleans, who pledged huge amounts of money to the Revolutionary War. Although the War was successful, Pollock lost much of his fortune and ended up bankrupt. It is in his many letters and records from 1778 requesting recompense from the government for his financial losses that we see his abbreviation for the Spanish peso rendered as the

$. Pollock may well have been one of many to use this abbreviation, but as his records are the ones that have survived it is to him that the creation of the dollar symbol has been attributed. The symbol caught on. A bond of 1792 signed by President George Washington provides what is thought to be the first official use of the symbol on an American financial document. By 1797 the first successful American type foundry, Binny & Ronaldson in Philadelphia, cast the first ever dollar sign for use in print, sealing its position as the 'official' symbol of the burgeoning American currency.

The dollar sign has become so inextricably linked to wealth that in modern times it is sometimes used typographically to imply greed by rendering a company name with a dollar sign in place of an *S*. It is also commonly used around the world as a motif to show a love of money or capitalism.

Euro sign

The idea for a joint currency for all of Europe was first mooted in the 1960s, but it was not until the 1990s that it finally became a reality. The name 'euro' was selected in 1995 in part because the word could be understood in all of the official European languages – a crucial attribute. The symbol that was to represent this new currency needed to be an easily recognized symbol of Europe, not to look out of place with existing currency symbols and to be easy to write. The brief was put out for tender to a number of unnamed teams and at least thirty design proposals were received.

The initial thirty designs were shortlisted to ten, which were put out for public consultation, whittling them down to a final two. President of the European Commission Jacques Santer and the commissioner in charge of economic and financial affairs, Yves-Thibault de Silguy, then selected the winning design. Their choice was unveiled to the public in December 1996, Santer presenting it to the press as a 5-metre-high symbol, enveloped in glass. The European Commission declared that the stylized *E* with two lines through it was inspired by the Greek letter epsilon – referring back to the birth of European civilization in Ancient Greece. The two lines bisecting the *E* were to denote the stability of the currency, and the shape as a whole was to evoke the *E* in Europe.

The European Commission revealed that four designers were behind the successful symbol but declined to name them. They also kept secret the identity of the runner-up, and indeed of all other entries in the competition, making the process seem rather mysterious.

On 1 January 1999 the euro came into being for use in electronic transfers; by 2001 banknotes and coins became available in all eleven member states. The banknotes carry the same design in every country. The coins have one common side, the other allowing for individual countries to add their own specific design – France chose a tree for its €1, symbolizing life, continuity and growth; Germany selected an eagle; Ireland went for the Celtic harp.

Shortly after the currency was released the foreign exchange company Travelex protested.

The European Commission had patented the symbol, making it the first currency symbol to be trademarked; this prompted Travelex to challenge them in court for trademark infringement, alleging that they had used a very similar symbol in their Interpayment Service division since 1989. The courts ultimately ruled in favour of the EC, but the intrigue surrounding the symbol's design did not end there. In 2001 the former chief graphic designer for the European Economic Community, Arthur Eisenmenger, piped up from his retirement home in Germany to reveal that he had in fact designed the euro symbol some twenty-five years before as a general symbol of Europe. His position was shored up by the fact that he had also been responsible for designing the star-ringed EU flag and the 'CE' used as a quality-control symbol across the European Union. Unwilling to reveal the names of the people they say designed the euro symbol, the European Commission remained largely silent on the controversy.

Although the euro symbol is a mere babe compared to other more august currency symbols, it has become instantly recognizable as an emblem of the European Union, representing a uniting force across the nineteen states of the Eurozone.

Copyright symbol

Copyright empowers the creator of an artistic, literary or other work to exert their rights as the owner of their work and prevent others from copying or distributing it without permission. The first copyright law was the Statute of Anne, introduced in Britain in 1710, which created a statutory right for authors. Since the introduction of the printing press in the fifteenth century the publishing trade had grown enormously, with thousands of books produced and circulated every year. As the trade flourished it became increasingly clear that some protection was needed for authors as any unscrupulous printer could copy and distribute their work without paying them a penny. The Statute of Anne was the solution, granting publishers fourteen years of legal protection for any published book. Once the fourteen years had passed the copyright would revert to the author for a further fourteen years. To ensure a work was protected it had to be registered by the Stationers' Company. Anyone breaking the copyright would be liable to a large fine and the destruction of their illegal copies. This was a groundbreaking law which not only recognized authors as the beneficiaries of copyright but also introduced the idea of it lasting for a set period of time. The law was influential and soon similar laws were passed in Denmark in 1741, in the United States in 1790 and in France in 1793.

By the nineteenth century, as publishing continued to expand internationally, it became clear that copyright needed to extend internationally. As a result, in 1886 in Berne, Switzerland, representatives of ten countries (including the UK) adopted the Berne Convention concerning the creation of an International Union for the Protection of Literary and Artistic Works, which gave creators the same minimum rights in all member countries of the Berne Union. Over the years the Berne Convention and other international treaties gave protection to a wide range of types of work in almost every country in the world, usually for between fifty and a hundred years.

Under the Berne Convention, copyright arises automatically when a work is created: no formalities for the grant of copyright, such as registration, are permitted. However, in some countries, notably the USA, formalities are considered essential. A notice of copyright on the work itself was first required by the US Copyright Act of 1802; it stated that the work should include the wording 'entered according to an act of Congress in the year — by [copyright holder's name] in the office of the Librarian of Congress, at Washington'. This was deemed rather lengthy, and so in a sop to artists they were allowed to add the information to the frame of their artwork rather than writing the whole thing out on the artwork itself. The revised Act of 1874 allowed the wording to be shortened to 'Copyright [insert year] by [insert name]' and this became standard. When discussions began for a new copyright act in America in the 1900s, artists and writers who were consulted on the plans requested that copyright be shown simply by adding their name to a work. Legislators, however, felt something more was needed and so in the 1909 iteration of the US Copyright Act they introduced the simple symbol of a *c* in a circle ©. At first the symbol could only be used on works of art such as paintings and photographs (where space was at a premium) rather than in books and periodicals, but in 1952 a new international treaty, the Universal Copyright

Convention, made its use, together with the year and the name of the creator, mandatory on literary and artistic works for which protection was sought in countries that were signatories of the UCC but not members of the Berne Union, such as the USA. The Berne Convention did not require the use of a copyright symbol; nevertheless its use spread around the world as it was essential for asserting creative rights in the huge US markets.

The USA finally joined the Berne Union in 1989. There are now 178 member states, and there is no country that is a signatory of the UCC that is not also a member of Berne. Consequently, the use of the copyright symbol is no longer a requirement anywhere in the world. It does nevertheless enjoy widespread use as a visual reminder to others that the work in question is covered by copyright laws, thereby ensuring that this neat little symbol continues to adorn artworks, books, articles, photographs, maps and numerous other pieces of creative output the world over.

Emoticons
& emoji

Although emoticons and emoji are, strictly speaking, not glyphs, this is the most sensible section in which to consider these phenomena, which have so impacted on modern communication.

As digital communication developed in the 1980s and 1990s a dichotomy soon emerged. Online chatrooms allowed for a more relaxed, informal conversational style; and yet without the attendant body language the tone of informality could be hard to gauge. As a result jokes were missed, people got offended and confusion abounded. To counteract this it was proposed that some form of easy way of adding emotion to a post be developed. The first person to suggest using the happy face :-) to show humorous or light-hearted content and the sad face :-(for serious content was computer scientist Scott Fahlman. He posted the idea on the Computer Science community message board at Carnegie Mellon in 1982 and it was immediately accepted.

His suggestion was especially successful because it utilized basic symbols available on every keyboard to create an instantly recognizable face (even if it required a head tilt to read it).

Fahlman's emoticons soon spread as people began using them in messages sent between universities, posting them on message boards and via email. Before long a whole host of emoticons had been developed to portray the full gamut of feeling, for example:

:-O	shock
;-)	nudge, nudge, wink, wink
:'(	crying
:-P	blowing raspberry
<3	heart
*<:-)	Father Christmas

The great thing about text-based emoticons is that they are easily drawn by anyone with a keyboard and so are simple to tack onto a message to convey feeling. However, over time more elaborate emoticons have developed; for example, the shrug ¯_(ツ)_/¯ which uses the *katakana* character *tsu* from Japanese to make the sideways smile facial expression. The word 'emoticon' itself – a portmanteau of 'emotion' and 'icon' – came into use around

1994. Today most word-processing programs will automatically convert a text-based smiling or sad-face emoticon into an emoji, indicating how quickly these new pictograms have inveigled their way into everyday communication, largely usurping the more simple emoticons. Emoji are now so readily available on most mobile-phone keyboards and built into social media messaging platforms that they have mostly taken over from where the emoticon began.

The very first emoji were designed by artist Shigetaka Kurita in 1999. Kurita had been commissioned by early mobile Internet platform 'i-mode', owned by Japanese mobile carrier Docomo, to create some visual images to communicate in simple form concepts such as the weather. Kurita came up with 176 original emoji, most of which were not people or emotions but pictograms to represent technology, transport, climate and love. The artwork for these original emoji are now housed in New York's Museum of Modern Art, attesting to their impact. Other Japanese mobile companies were soon copying Docomo's idea, realizing the versatility of the emoji. Users quickly embraced them as a way to add colour, personality and warmth to an otherwise sterile method of communication.

Where Japan led, the rest of the world followed, and before long emoji were cropping up on mobile phones across the globe.

Emoji is a loanword from Japanese created from *e*, meaning 'picture', and *moji*, which means 'character' or 'letter'. In 2007 Google decided to try to formalize the emoji and lobbied the Unicode Consortium (the not-for-profit organization that oversees text standards across all computers) to have it accepted as standard Unicode. Finally in October 2010 the first emoji were accepted into Unicode, meaning that they could be used on any operating system across the world – this meant that if you were texting on an Apple phone the emoji you typed would still show up if received on an Android device. By now the emoji had incorporated a whole host of human expressions, professions, characters and costumes, becoming a visual language all of its own. As emoji are used more widely across the world it has become even more important that the images reflect the many and varied cultures of the globe. To this end you can now select any number of skin tones or hair colours for your smiling face; different religions are represented with turbans, the hijab and prayer-bead emoji. Initial gender gaps in the representations of certain professions have also been addressed, with both male and female doctor emoji now available, for instance. To keep emoji up to date and inclusive the Unicode Consortium emoji subcommittee meets twice a week to consider new proposals. Anyone can propose a new emoji, but they must justify its need to be created and suggest how it might look. Once the subcommittee approves a new emoji it can take up to two years for it to be written into Unicode. In 2019 some of the newest emoji accepted into Unicode were: a sloth, a guide dog, a waffle, a Hindu temple and a same-sex couple.

Emoji are now fully mainstream and are deployed millions of times a day in all quarters of digital communication. They have become so accepted that there is an unofficial World Emoji Day (17 July) to celebrate their usage. In 2015 the 'face with tears of joy' was designated a 'word' of the year by Oxford Dictionaries, in part because it was the most used emoji of that year. In 2017 *The Emoji Movie* was released. The beauty of the emoji is its simplicity. A pictogram can communicate a concept or a feeling with ease, regardless of language barriers, helping us to add some much-needed warmth to our digital communication.

Mathematical symbols

> So Mathematical Truth prefers simple words
> since the language of Truth is itself simple.
>
> Tycho Brahe, *Epistolarum astronomicarum
> liber primus*, 1596

Across the world people have always had to deal with numbers and counting when farming, trading, building and cooking – to name just a few activities. This has meant that counting and numbering systems have developed in numerous ways. Early counting was primarily done through tallying. For example, in the Highlands of Scotland before battle each warrior would place a stone on the cairn. After battle each surviving soldier would remove a stone from the cairn, the resulting pile providing not only a count of the casualties but also a memorial to their fallen comrades. Objects close to hand, such as fingers, stones, shells and twigs, can all be used to tally, creating a visual representation of a number.

Over time, tallies developed into more complex methods such as notching stones or bones, tying knots in strings of different lengths or colours, and making marks on wooden posts. As these tallies became more complex people began to count in groups of numbers, probably first in twos, then in fives, then tens and twenties, making larger amounts easier to record. As the written word became an important method of communication, there came a conceptual leap whereby the objects being counted could be represented by a numeral, rather than by the physical number of objects themselves.

The Ancient Egyptians created one of the earliest numerical systems around 3000 BCE. Similar systems subsequently emerged in Greece and in the Roman world. The Romans developed Roman numerals, which were the dominant way to write numbers across Europe until they were gradually superseded by the Hindu–Arabic numerals towards the end of the fourteenth century. For hundreds of years there were numbers but no further symbols to represent mathematical equations. This meant that many early mathematicians wrote out their equations in words in rhetorical fashion. But for even quite simple equations the sentences could go on and on. For example, in Euclid's *Elements* (*c.* 300 BCE), one of the founding texts of Western mathematics, there are no symbols other than letters which stand for points, double letters for lines and triple letters for angles.

As mathematical knowledge grew, it became more and more cumbersome to have to write out long sentences to explain an arithmetical problem. Increasingly, by the seventeenth century shorthand symbols were being used instead. Inevitably, consensus on which symbols to use for which function was slow to build and competing symbols coexisted. The key driver for one symbol achieving ascendancy often came down not to its utility but to its being promoted by an especially famous mathematician.

Thomas Hobbes in 1648 bemoaned the increasing shift towards the use of symbols in geometry: 'Symbols are poor unhandsome, though necessary scaffolds of demonstration … though they shorten the writing, yet they do not make the reader understand it sooner than if it were written in words.' This may have been true during the infancy of mathematical symbols, but today, through hundreds of years of use, modern mathematical symbols are very effective in communicating mathematical concepts in shorthand. Mathematical notation is like a language in itself, the symbols holding distinct meanings, which when used in certain sequences can communicate whole theorems and concepts.

OZero

The absence of a value is a complex concept, one that many ancient civilizations struggled with. Romans and Egyptians had no numeral to represent zero. The Mayan number system did have a glyph to represent the idea of zero but it never left their empire. The Ancient Sumerians were the first to develop a method of counting in order to record the number of livestock in account books; however, the system was positional, meaning that where a mark was placed in relation to other marks revealed its amount. The Sumerian system was passed down to the Babylonians from about 2000 BCE and they created a symbol to represent nothingness (two small wedge shapes), but it was used more as a placeholder than as a numeral.

Numerous locations for the birth of a recognizable zero have been proposed over the years, but the scholarship indicates that the issue is unlikely ever to be resolved. One early zero was uncovered in 1931 by George Cœdès, a French academic. This was inscribed on a stone stele on a temple near Angkor Wat, Cambodia. The inscription is dated 605 (providing the zero); as the Cambodian calendar began in 78 CE, this dates the inscription to 683 CE. During the turbulent years of the Khmer Rouge the inscription was lost, but it was thankfully rediscovered in 2013 by mathematician Amir Aczel and went on display at the National Museum of Cambodia in 2017.

In September 2017 scholars argued for the discovery of an even earlier zero in an ancient Indian mathematical text known as the Bakhshali manuscript, which is held at Oxford's Bodleian Library. Radiocarbon dating indicated that this manuscript was produced as early as the third or fourth century CE, although there is some debate about this analysis. The manuscript itself, which was discovered buried in a field in 1881 in what is today Pakistan, is written on seventy delicate leaves of birch bark. Historians believe it represents a training manual for Silk Road traders, teaching them concepts of arithmetic.

The previous earliest Indian example of a zero has been dated to the ninth century; it was found inscribed on a temple in Gwalior. Curators at the

Bodleian Library explained the importance of the find: 'the symbol in the Bakhshali manuscript is particularly significant for two reasons. Firstly, it is this dot that evolved to have a hollow centre and became the symbol that we use as zero today. Secondly, it was only in India that this zero developed into a number in its own right, hence creating the concept and the number zero that we understand today.'

Not all scholars accept this reading of the Bakhshali zero. However, the majority agree that the round symbol with a hole that we recognize as zero did originate in India. Later, in the seventh century CE, it was the Indian mathematician Brahmagupta who began using small dots under numbers to represent a zero placeholder. Furthermore, he used the concept of *sunya* to reveal the null value of a zero – the value you get when you subtract a number from itself. By 773 CE, in Baghdad, Muḥammad ibn Mūsā al-Khwārizmī (after whom the algorithm is named) demonstrated how zero (which he called *sifr*) could be used in algebraic equations. When Italian mathematician Leonardo of Pisa, better known as Fibonacci, brought al-Khwārizmī's work to Italy in the early thirteenth century he helped to popularize Arabic numerals. Fibonacci built on this work in his book *Liber Abaci*, the 'Book of Counting', which was published in 1202, and introduced many Arabic mathematical concepts (such as zero) to Europeans for the first time. The Italian authorities, however, became concerned that these new numbers could be easily corrupted and changed, and as a result they were outlawed. Despite this, merchants found the concept of zero so useful that they continued to use the numbers in secret encrypted messages. In this way the Arabic word for zero, *sifr*, was adopted in Europe to mean zero and later was used to refer to any numeral. Because numerals were often used in early codes, the word *sifr* gradually became corrupted to 'cipher' and gave us our word for code.

As zero emerged into the mainstream it continued to present mathematicians with a complex problem: how do you divide by zero? In the early seventeenth century both German polymath Gottfried Wilhelm Leibniz and Sir Isaac Newton tussled with this problem and independently came to similar conclusions. Their work led to the development of calculus (in which the summation of infinitesimal differences are calculated), which went on to form the basis of modern physics, engineering and economics. Zero, then, has a long history of development, with many of the greatest minds of Asia, Africa and Europe building on the swell of knowledge to fully understand the significance of the absence of value.

Plus sign

The concept of addition has been in use the world over ever since ideas of counting were first developed. Addition is vital for farmers and traders to keep track of their stock. Prior to the thirteenth century calculations were mostly written out in full sentences and so mathematical symbols were not employed, or at least did not become universal. Exceptions can be found, however. The Rhind Papyrus (named after Scottish Egyptologist Alexander Henry Rhind, who purchased it in 1858, though it was copied by a scribe named Ahmes and is sometimes more correctly known as the Ahmes Papyrus) is one such example. The papyrus was written in hieratic, a cursive form of hieroglyphics, during the Egyptian Second Intermediate Period $c.1700-c.1550$ BCE. The manuscript is a compendium of mathematical problems, giving basic calculations and exercises – for example, for working out the volume of a cylinder. The Rhind

Papyrus employs the visual symbol of a pair of legs walking towards a number to indicate addition and legs walking away to indicate subtraction. This is one of the earliest known examples of a symbol being used to suggest addition.

In general, in early mathematical texts addition is demonstrated by the juxtaposition of the numbers in question. Similarly in most early Indian mathematical manuscripts, although operations of addition are written out, no symbol for addition is found. In the Bakhshali manuscript, from the third or fourth century CE, addition is denoted with the word *yu* (short for *yuta*, meaning 'increased').

Most historians agree that the plus sign, as we recognize it today, first began appearing in European texts in the fourteenth century. French astronomer Nicole Oresme (1323–1382) has been proposed as the first person to use the plus sign as a shortening of the Latin word *et*, 'and', in his book *Algorismus proportionum*. The shortening is found in a copy of his book made in the latter part of the fourteenth century, but the abbreviation may have been created by the copyist and might not have appeared in Oresme's original text, written *c.* 1351–5, so he cannot officially be credited with the creation of the sign.

French mathematician Nicolas Chuquet, in 1484, and Italian mathematician Luca Pacioli, in 1494, used the letter *p* with a straight line over the top, or a plain *p*, to denote plus; some argue that this sign could have later morphed into the + sign. The first definite plus and minus signs to be committed to the printed page appear in Johannes Widmann's *Mercantile Arithmetic*, published in Leipzig in 1489. But they did not represent addition and subtraction; rather, they were used to show surpluses or deficits in a business context.

Giel Vander Hoecke, a Dutch mathematician, is thought to be the first person to use the plus and minus signs in algebra, in 1514, in his book *Een sonderlinghe boeck in dye edel conste arithmetica*, published in Antwerp. *Arithmetica Integra* (1544), by German Michael Stifel (1487–1567), was an early European text that used the plus and minus symbols. This book was popular across Europe and so would have helped to assure the place of the two symbols with their correct meanings.

Robert Recorde was the first to use the plus and minus signs in a printed book in England in his *The Whetstone of Witte* (1557). He wrote of the symbols: 'There be other 2 signes in often use of which the first is made thus + and betokeneth more: the other is thus made – and betokeneth lesse.' Recorde was a very influential mathematician and so his use of the symbols would have encouraged their more general adoption in Britain. The Italians continued to use p and m to represent plus and minus well into the sixteenth century, a confusion of symbols that was reflected in France and Spain, where the German plus and minus and the Italian p and m were both used. It was not always down to personal choice which symbols were used. For example, the Spanish mathematician Juan Pérez de Moya used the Italian symbols in his 1562 book *Diálogos de aritmética práctica y especulativa* for the reason that 'These characters I am moved to adopt, because others are not to be had in the printing office.' The German + and – competed with the Italian p and m throughout the sixteenth century, with the + and – finally becoming dominant across Europe by the early seventeenth century after being adopted by the most influential mathematicians. Hence it was not necessarily the utility of the symbol that assured its widespread acceptance but rather its adoption and promotion in widely circulated mathematical texts.

Minus sign

The history of the minus sign is hard to trace because it is essentially the same symbol as a dash or hyphen (see page 56) in written English. A number of theories about the origin of the sign abound, but none can be verified. Some say it derived from the bar sign, known as *minus*, that merchants used to separate the tare, the empty weight of the container used for shipping goods, and the weight of the goods supplied.

Diophantus in *Arithmetica* created a minus sign which looked a little like an arrow pointing upwards. He called this concept 'wanting'. The original text of *Arithmetica* does not survive, so any symbol notations may be later additions by scribes. Little is known of Diophantus, but it is thought he flourished in the third century CE. Originally thirteen books made up *Arithmetica*, but only six have survived as copies of the original Greek text. Today most scholars base their understanding of the text on a Latin translation copied in about 1545. The manuscript was repeatedly copied from the original Greek to Arabic and Aramaic over hundreds of years, so it is inevitable that errors will have crept into the text. The abbreviations we attribute to Diophantus could easily have been added by any number of rogue scribes over the years, and they cannot be dated.

In the mid-fifteenth century in France and Italy the concept of 'taking away' was indicated with the letter *m*, for minus. But at roughly the same time the short bar sign was being used to represent minus in Germany, and, as with the plus sign, it first appeared in print in Johannes Widmann's *Mercantile Arithmetic* (1489). A minus sign has been found in an earlier manuscript in Dresden Library written in 1481; here it is used in an algebraic equation. It is known that Widmann, who lectured at the University of Leipzig, studied this manuscript (and left annotations in the margins); so, although he is credited with producing the first minus sign in print, he clearly did not invent the sign himself but rather adopted and popularized it.

It was not a steady ascendance for the minus sign; it had to see off competition from alternative symbols. During the fifteenth and sixteenth centuries both *m* and the – sign appeared across Europe to denote subtraction, but some mathematicians also occasionally used what today we would recognize as the divide sign ÷. Additionally, in the seventeenth century René Descartes and Marin Mersenne both employed a series of two or three dots. It seems likely that alternatives were proposed in an effort to reduce confusion. The – sign was widely used in punctuation as a hyphen and was also used in other mathematical contexts, such as by Widmann to separate terms in proportion. This lack of clarity and confusion with other existing symbols and meanings meant that it took longer for a consensus to be reached on the symbol for subtraction than was achieved with other mathematical symbols. Indeed in some Scandinavian mathematical texts the divide sign was still used in subtraction up until the early twentieth century.

The minus sign is also now used to show negative numbers. This concept of a number that is less than zero, which is often required where a scale exists, for example in temperature, was first understood by the Chinese during the Han dynasty (202 BCE–220 CE). Negative numbers first appear in the Chinese text *Nine Chapters on the Mathematical Arts*, which may itself be based on an older work.

Indian mathematicians such as Brahmagupta were also describing negative numbers in the seventh century CE. But in Britain negative numbers were deemed absurd and largely ignored. English mathematician Francis Maseres, for example, wrote in 1758 of negative numbers that they 'darken the very whole doctrines of the equations and make dark of the things which are in their nature excessively obvious and simple'. It took until the mid-nineteenth century, when Augustus De Morgan and George Peacock's work on algebra called for negative numbers to be accepted, that they were finally recognized as a concept in Britain and signified by placing a minus sign in front of the number. And so it has been a long journey for – to signify minus, although it really only gains its meaning in context. A plus sign by itself would be recognized as such; however, a minus sign on its own could easily be taken for a dash, proving that not all mathematical symbols hold their meaning outside the correct context.

Multiply symbol

The concept of multiplication developed as people began to count. Multiplication used by early civilizations such as the Babylonians relied on adding repeatedly or doubling. These calculations were generally written out in lines of numbers and multiplication was signified by juxtaposition, so a symbol was not required. Although other methods were proposed – for example, Michael Stifel used the letter m to denote multiplication in 1545 – juxtaposition continued to be the most commonly used method until the seventeenth century when suddenly a number of symbols were proposed.

Two rival symbols for multiplication developed concurrently, the central dot and the × sign. In Thomas Harriot's *Artis Analyticae Praxis* (1631) multiplication was shown by the use of a dot, but at the same time William Oughtred in *Clavis Mathematicæ* (1631) used the × symbol. Scholars believe that Oughtred first used the × symbol in

1618 in an anonymous appendix to Edward Wright's translation of John Napier's *Descriptio*; this suggests that the use of the × slightly precedes that of the dot. Oughtred used the St Andrew's cross to show multiplication, but others used the letter *x* to the same effect. The St Andrew's cross was found in some earlier medieval manuscripts as part of mathematical notation, but it was used for a variety of different meanings, including adding and subtracting fractions. However, it was Oughtred who first used it in direct relation to multiplication.

When tracing the history of symbols used for mathematical equations we need to be conscious of the role played by typesetters. In Descartes's *La Géométrie* (1637) he occasionally used the German cross to represent multiplication. It is not clear if he chose this symbol himself or if the typesetter, unable to find a letter punch corresponding to the notation Descartes actually used, utilized an existing one.

Competing symbols continued to be used well into the 1800s. Johann Rahn in 1659 in *Teutsche Algebra* employed an asterisk to show multiplication. G.W. Leibniz used a dot, writing in a letter of 29 July 1698 'I do not like × as a symbol for multiplication, as it is easily confounded with *x*.' In 1710 the Berlin Academy published a work promoting Leibniz's symbols and stating that multiplication should be shown via apposition or by a dot or comma; the St Andrew's cross was deemed to be the least preferable option.

Although the dot persisted in some regions, with both Christian Wolf and Euler favouring it for multiplication, in England Oughtred's × was most commonly used and has endured. The × for multiplication is the symbol taught in British schools and is found on calculators. However, in more advanced maths and algebra, brevity is key; and so most frequently in this context multiplication is currently shown either with a dot or by juxtaposition, in an echo back to the earliest written multiplication sums.

The similarity of the × to the symbol for an unknown number or variable x has caused difficulties as computing programming has developed. In 1960 American Standard Code for Information Interchange (ASCII) was developed from telegraphic codes and was initially used for teleprinting by Bell data services. The first ASCII code had no separate symbol for a variable so it was impossible to write out the calculation $x \times y$. Consequently in ASCII an asterisk was used to denote multiplication, so the sum could be written x * y and confusion could be avoided. This device has largely continued in computer programming.

Due to the many different contexts in which the multiply symbol is used, from teaching basic mathematics to schoolchildren right up to programming the most complex algebra problems, it has developed in a number of guises, each of which has persisted in its own context.

Divide symbol

The divide symbol is known as an obelus – confusingly the name also given to the dagger symbol. The symbol first appeared in 1525 in the work of German mathematician Adam Ries; however, it was used not to show division but in place of a minus sign in arithmetic. (This usage was not uncommon: the sign continued to be employed in some contexts to show subtraction right up until the early twentieth century.)

The galley method of division is the oldest known way to write out and solve division and was the most widely used method until the seventeenth century. Some historians trace its origin to Chinese mathematicians in the first century CE, while others find its roots in ninth-century Arab mathematics. The method writes out the problem long form and as the sum progresses the numbers begin to take on a boat shape, hence the name 'galley'. By the sixteenth century, European mathematicians began to develop long division, which as a method has been credited to English mathematician Henry Briggs, who wrote it down in 1597. This method similarly does not use a symbol; instead a line is used to separate the numbers.

As sums increasingly began to be written out in notation in the seventeenth century, a series of different symbols developed to denote division. For some a colon was used; this can be seen in the work of William Oughtred (1574–1660). Others utilized the ever-handy slash /. But in 1659 Swiss mathematician Johann Rahn used the obelus to denote division in his book *Teutsche Algebra*. An English translation of his work in 1668, with some additions by John Pell, brought the symbol to England where it was soon accepted (although largely credited to Pell). It later spread to America and other English-speaking countries.

On the Continent, however, the colon persisted as the symbol of division and was favoured by influential German polymath G.W. Leibniz (1646–1716). Christian Wolf likewise popularized across Germany the colon for division and the dot for multiplication with his use of the symbols in his textbooks. Use of the colon persisted in continental Europe and South America. This geographical and language-based divide continued. In 1923 the National Committee on Mathematical Requirements wrote: 'Since neither ÷ nor :, as signs of division, plays any part in business life, it seems proper to consider only the needs of algebra, and to make more use of the fractional form and (where the meaning is clear) of the symbol /, and to drop the symbol ÷ in writing algebraic expressions.'

The standard computer keyboard includes a plus, a minus and an equals sign, but it does not have an obelus (you must dive into the 'special characters' to insert one), even though English school books still make use of it. It does, however, feature the multipurpose slash.

Equals sign

Traditionally in Europe most arithmetic was written out rhetorically in long form and in Latin, as this was the dominant language of scholarship. This meant that 'is equal to' was generally written as *aequales* or sometimes shortened to *aeq*. In 1557 Welsh mathematician Robert Recorde was the first to use the = sign to show equality, when he wrote: 'And to avoide the tediouse repetition of these woordes: is equalle to: I will sette as I doe often in woorke use, a paire of paralleles, of Gemowe [twin] lines of one lengthe.' He added: 'Noe 2 thynges can be moare equalle.' These parallel lines (drawn longer than those we use today) appeared in his book on arithmetic and algebra *The Whetstone of Witte* (1557). Recorde was something of a polymath, writing numerous textbooks over the years, on everything from urine to the abacus. The important fact about his books is that, rather than being written in Latin, they were written in vernacular English, meaning they were accessible to a far wider readership.

This symbol did not immediately become standard; others continued to be used. Humanist scholar Wilhelm Xylander (1532–1576), for example, preferred two upright parallel lines. Descartes, for his part, introduced in *La Géométrie* (1637) a sign resembling half an infinity symbol (or a looped piece of thread on its side); this was also commonly used, into the 1700s, to denote equality. However, in 1631 Recorde's symbol was used in a number of influential texts, including William Oughtred's *Clavis Mathematicæ*, Richard Norwood's *Trigonometrie* and Thomas Harriot's *Artis Analyticae Praxis*. It is unclear why there was suddenly such a groundswell in favour of one particular symbol, some seventy years after it had first been proposed, but its appearance in these popular texts gave his symbol the edge over other contenders.

In England, at least, the use of parallel lines as an equals symbol was fully accepted when Sir Isaac Newton adopted it. Newton's work was widely circulated in Europe and no doubt helped Recorde's symbol gain traction against its European rivals, led by the Cartesian looped symbol. Not one to hold a grudge, Descartes himself used Recorde's symbol in a letter of 1640, suggesting he was not averse to its use. In Germany G.W. Leibniz was also an early adopter of Recorde's symbol, in about 1683, and his influence ensured it began to be used in Germany.

Leonhard Euler (1707–1783) introduced a symbol to denote 'not equal' which looks like an equals sign with a diagonal line through it ≠. By creating a sign based on the equals sign itself, Euler helped to make the original more widely accepted. By the eighteenth century Recorde's symbol had become established across most of Europe. Its simplicity and utility endured, making it one of just a few mathematical symbols that have become universal.

Greater than
& less than

The signs for greater than > and less than <, also known as signs of inequality, were first seen in print in English mathematician Thomas Harriot's book *Artis Analyticae Praxis*, which was published in 1631, ten years after his death. Consequently the symbols have been credited to him. However, analysis of his original manuscript show that Harriot actually used hand-drawn triangles on their sides, and so it has been concluded that the symbols were introduced by his editor. (Similarly the printed edition of Harriot's book used the recently introduced equals sign = where in his manuscript Harriot used the alternative symbol of two equal vertical lines II.) This is a clear example of the typesetter or editor selecting for use in printing a symbol that has then been attributed to the author. In the long history of the development of symbols it is likely that this happened many times; however, given that the dialogue between writer and typesetter or editor has rarely been preserved, we can only make assumptions from the printed record. This disconnect between the author's usage and the printed version can only become apparent if the original manuscript survives, as is the case with Harriot.

The greater than and less than symbols are rarely used alone, as their meaning only becomes clear through their juxtaposition with the numerals on either side of them, for example $4 > 3$ (four is greater than three). Many people struggle with the way round the symbols should be written, so in schools children are often taught to see the symbols as crocodiles with gaping mouths. Naturally crocodiles always want to eat the bigger number, so the open mouth will always face this. When writing out inequality, if you bear this visual trick in mind you should always get the symbol the correct way round.

In 1734 French mathematician Pierre Bouguer added to the pantheon of mathematical symbols by introducing the symbols for 'greater than or equals to' and 'less than or equals to'. He selected a neat portmanteau of the equals symbol and the existing greater than and less than signs to create $\leq$ and $\geq$. These symbols helped further clarify the writing out of inequality. In a case of over-egging the pudding, Leonhard Euler (1707–1783) also used a symbol for 'not equal to, not greater than, not less than'. It is unclear if Euler invented the symbol – which looks like the greater than symbol but with a line running horizontally through the middle – or if he was adopting an existing one; his use of this somewhat niche symbol is evident in his correspondence with fellow mathematician Christian Goldbach.

Per cent

A percentage is a number expressed as a fraction of 100. This concept has been in use since at least Ancient Roman times. The emperor Augustus was thought to have introduced the *centesima rerum venalium* tax, which literally means a hundredth of the value of everything sold; it was used as a 1 per cent tax on items sold at auction. This was long before the system of decimal fractions was developed, but it meant Roman traders became familiar with computing these. At this point percentages were expressed long form in Latin as *per centum* (by the hundred).

In fifteenth-century Italy, as denominations of money grew, it became more common for merchants and traders to use computations with a denominator of 100; frequent references to this are found in texts of the period. Per cent was at first shown as a variety of abbreviations, such as *p cento*, *per 100* or *p 100*. At the same time scribes began using a line slashed through the descender of the letter p to indicate that it was an abbreviation meaning 'per'.

In 1908 the president of the Mathematical Association of America, David Eugene Smith, was cataloguing fifteenth-century Italian manuscripts when he came across an Italian text from $c.$ 1435 in which he found a new abbreviation for per cent, which he suspected might be the ancestor of our modern symbol. This abbreviation had a p followed by a c, with a superscript o – pc^o. The p and c were obvious abbreviations of *per centum* and it is thought the superscript o is likely to represent the o from the end of Italian ordinals, as in *primo* (first) or *secondo* (second), much like in English when we use 'st' 'nd' or 'th' to represent English ordinals.

Smith proposed that it was from this early abbreviation that the modern % derived, citing a further Italian text from 1694 to illustrate his point. In this document the p had become an elaborate initial, the c had become a closed circle with a horizontal line above it, over which the superscript o rested, making it a closer approximation of the modern per cent sign. It is thought that over time the p was dropped, leaving just the symbol, which slowly developed into the more stylized version in use today.

As denominations have grown ever larger the per mille symbol ‰ was developed to show a fraction of 1,000, and the permyriad ‱ to show a fraction of 10,000. Publishers' style guides generally advise that the per cent symbol be eschewed in favour of writing out the word in full – in British English as 'per cent' and in American English as 'percent'. It is generally agreed that where the symbol is to be used, there should be no space between the numeral and the symbol, as in 5%.

Degree symbol

Geographer and astronomer Claudius Ptolemy (*c.* 100–170 CE) was one of the earliest thinkers to write about degrees, stating that there were 360 degrees in a circle (an idea originating in Babylonian astronomy) and 60 minutes in a degree. However, when writing out his measurements or calculations, he did not use the symbol that is familiar today. It was not until the 1569 edition of *Arithmeticae practicae methodus facilis* by Gemma Frisius (1508–1555) that the familiar symbol of a raised zero appeared in print for the first time. The symbol developed from the sexagesimal division of a degree into 60 minutes (of arc) and one minute as 60 seconds (of arc), which is used to give greater accuracy in coordinates for astronomy and geography. Notation written like this is known as DMS – for degrees, minutes, seconds. In this notation minutes were originally shown as a superscript Roman numeral for I and seconds as superscript

Roman II, and so it made sense for the degrees to be shown with a superscript zero. Over time Roman numerals were replaced with ´ for minutes and ˝ for seconds. Erasmus Reinhold went on to use the same system of ° ´ ˝ for degrees, minutes, seconds in the edition of *Prutenicae tabulae coelestium motuum* published in 1571, seemingly sealing this notation into common usage.

The invention of the degree symbol was initially used for geometry when measuring angles (although in most other mathematical disciplines the radian is used to measure angles) and in giving coordinates. When in 1714 Daniel Gabriel Fahrenheit developed the first accurate mercury thermometer, and in 1724 the temperature scale that bears his name, the degree symbol was adopted to indicate the temperature measurement. For example, in the Fahrenheit scale 212°F is the boiling point of water. Likewise, when Swedish astronomer Anders Celsius introduced his alternative temperature scale in 1742 the degree symbol was adopted for notation. Incidentally, Celsius actually developed his scale opposite to the way we use it today, with zero as the boiling point of water and 100 as the freezing point. It was Swedish botanist and taxonomist extraordinaire Carl Linnaeus (1707–1778) who inverted the scale when he had a custom-made thermometer built for his glasshouse in 1744. The scale this way round made more sense and it soon caught on across Europe.

In contrast, when the Kelvin scale was developed by Lord Kelvin in 1848 to show extremes of hot and cold, it too was initially noted with a degree symbol. However, in 1967 at the 13th General Conference of Weights and Measures in Paris it was decided that while the degree symbol was good for expressing temperature on a relative scale such as Fahrenheit and Celsius, for a more accurate scale like Kelvin it did not cut the mustard. This is because on the Kelvin scale each measurement represents an actual measure of thermal energy as the scale is based on absolute zero – the point at which gas molecules have no thermal energy – at the bottom. So from 1967 the Kelvin scale ceased to use the degree symbol and is expressed simply as K.

Pi

Pi is the ratio of the circumference of any circle to the diameter of that circle. No matter how large or small the circle, pi will always be the same. In Ancient Greece, the great mathematician Archimedes (287–212 BCE) pondered the problem. He used a series of polygons within the circle to create a calculation that could offer a close approximation of pi. Chinese mathematician Zu Chongzhi (429–500 CE) got closer still to calculating pi. The issue continued to beguile and fascinate mathematicians across the globe. In the sixteenth century mathematicians were still using versions of Archimedes' polygon technique to calculate pi. In 1596 Dutch mathematician Ludolph van Ceulen used the technique to calculate pi to twenty decimal places by using polygons with over 500 million sides. This was the start of a lifelong obsession for van Ceulen, who continued to work on calculations until his death in 1610, by which point he had accurately determined thirty-five decimal places. The work of van Ceulen was so revered by his contemporaries that his calculation of pi was inscribed on his gravestone in St Peter's Churchyard in Leiden (the original tombstone was unfortunately lost, but it was re-created in 2000).

The symbol to represent pi π first appeared in Oughtred's *Clavis Mathematicæ* in 1631, but there it was applied to show the circumference of a circle – this meant that it was not a constant but a number that changed depending on the size of the circle. It is thought Oughtred chose this symbol because during this period the circumference of a circle was known as 'periphery' and so the Greek letter π was deemed a good abbreviation.

In 1706 the pi symbol was first used to denote the ratio of the circumference of a circle to its diameter by Welsh self-taught mathematician William Jones in his second book *Synopsis Palmariorum Matheseos*. Jones had acquired a number of Oughtred's books and notes from John Collins (1625–1683), who had himself inherited them from Oughtred's library. Jones suspected but could not prove that pi was an irrational number, meaning that it was an infinite non-repeating decimal, which therefore could never be written out fully. As a consequence Jones decided to use the pi symbol, previously employed by Oughtred, to represent the ratio of the circumference of a circle to its diameter. This proved to be a grand conceptual leap in mathematical thinking.

Leonhard Euler went on to popularize the π symbol, first using it in 1737 and then by including it in his influential *Introductio in analysin infinitorum* (1748). In 1761 Johann Heinrich Lambert (1728–1777) provided the proof that Jones had been lacking and confirmed that pi was indeed an irrational number. A further leap in understanding of pi came in 1882 when Ferdinand von Lindemann offered proof that pi was transcendental, which basically means it is not the solution to any algebraic equations. The proof showed that a circle cannot be squared.

As calculation methods improved, the value of pi was calculated to more and more decimal places – by the start of the twentieth century pi was known to around 500 digits, and in 1973 it was calculated to 1 million digits. Modern computers have pushed knowledge of pi to ever greater limits. To date the value of pi has been calculated to over a trillion digits – an unimaginably enormous value.

Infinity

The concept of infinity has captivated mathematicians for thousands of years. The Ancient Greeks saw infinity as a messy, dangerous thing, as referenced by their word for it, *apeiron*, which means 'unbounded'. The chaos from which the modern world was born was *apeiron*. But mathematics is stalked by the limitless possibilities of infinity and it became a problem that many minds tussled over. Infinity became divided into two concepts: potential infinity and actual infinity. Potential infinity could be, for example, the sequence of positive integers, 1, 2, 3, 4 and so on, which can go on indefinitely and yet is formed of definite numbers reached by adding one each time. The numbers are countable, but the counting process would never end. Actual infinity relates to something, such as a set, with a definite start and end point but with an infinite quantity of numbers or 'things' within it. For example, a line has a start and end point but an uncountable number of points in between, as in theory the line could be endlessly magnified, giving an ever-increasing number of points.

Historians' understanding of the development of the notion of infinity was given a boost in 2011 when an ancient manuscript by Archimedes was finally deciphered. The manuscript, known as the Archimedes Palimpsest, had first been discovered in 1906 by Danish Archimedes scholar Johan Ludvig Heiberg. The Byzantine prayer book had been created in the thirteenth century using earlier manuscripts which were scraped off and written over. Heiberg noticed that underneath a number of pages were traces of writings by Archimedes which had been copied out by scribes in Constantinople in the tenth century. It was fiendishly difficult to make out the words and the manuscript was soon sold into private hands. In 1998 it suddenly reappeared for sale at Christie's New York, unfortunately in even worse condition than before. An anonymous American collector purchased the Palimpsest for $2 million and generously deposited it at Baltimore's Walters Art Museum where it could be studied. By 2011 technology had advanced enough that, using the latest multispectral imaging and X-ray techniques, the contents of Archimedes' treatise could be read. Mathematicians were astonished to find that Archimedes, in the third century BCE, was working on the concept of infinity, many hundreds of years before it was thought to have originally been explored. And so these traces of Archimedes' work have transformed modern ideas of how infinity as a concept developed.

John Wallis (1616–1703) was a clergyman and mathematician who in the seventeenth century began working on ideas of infinity. His work has been credited as laying the foundation for later developments in infinitesimal calculus. In his 1655 work *Tractatus de sectionibus conicis* Wallis used the first infinity symbol in print ∞, alongside a description of its meaning, immediately linking the two. Wallis did not explain why he decided on this symbol, but it is thought that he may have been inspired either by the Roman symbol for 1,000, CIↃ, or by the last letter of the Greek alphabet, omega ω. It has also been noted that the symbol resembles a number 8 on its side, as well as the ancient motif the ouroboros, a serpent eating its own tail, both of which have no beginning or end. Several rival symbols for infinity were proposed; for example, Euler used an open infinity symbol, like an *s* lying on its side, and German mathematician Georg

Cantor (1845–1918) used the symbol for the first letter of the Hebrew alphabet, aleph א (although this had a more specific meaning). However, the pleasing looped shape of Wallis's infinity symbol, which so readily encapsulates its meaning, was the symbol that caught on in mathematics and beyond.

The symbol might have remained in its niche, familiar to just mathematicians and calculus fans, had it not been picked up by mystics. By the early eighteenth century the infinity symbol began making an appearance on the tarot card of the Magus or Juggler. In some depictions the character is also shown wearing an ouroboros belt. In this context infinity is used to show that there can be no beginning without an end, and no end without a beginning, and speaks of the eternal nature of the human spirit. By taking the symbol outside its mathematical confines it began to be used more widely to represent eternity and as a signifier of empowerment. Consequently, today people sport infinity symbols as tattoos and give jewellery embossed with the symbol to denote the eternal nature of their love.

Endangered & extinct symbols

Yea, all things live forever, though
at times they sleep and are forgotten.

H. Rider Haggard, *She*, 1886

The symbols gathered here are only grouped together because they share the ignoble status of being under threat of endangerment or extinction. In the long history of the written word a number of symbols and punctuation marks have developed which have served competing functions; and there are many that have fallen by the wayside.

Henry Denham in 1580 proposed the creation of the percontation mark, a back-to-front question mark, which he argued should be used to identify a rhetorical question. For reasons unknown (or maybe simply because it wasn't actually a good idea), Denham's percontation mark never caught on. Likewise the asterism, a natty symbol created from a triangulation of three asterisks, was for a time used as a reference or footnote mark, but it failed to find a popular foothold. And dare we even mention the various attempts to create a mark that communicates irony? The most recent (2010) was the controversial (patented, no less) SarcMark, with which Paul and Douglas J. Sak tried to monetize the use of irony by charging people to download their symbol to roll out every time they wanted to signpost that they were being sarcastic.

The invented symbols that have failed to catch on show how hard it is for a new mark to gain and maintain common usage. Notably, many symbols have teetered on the edge of extinction (see *Hash sign* and *At sign*), before they were pulled from the abyss and repurposed, giving them a new lease of life. The symbols included here were all at one time widely deployed and understood, but for one reason or another their meaning and purpose have diminished. Some, like the poor pilcrow, have been effectively replaced by a blank space; others, like the Tironian *et*, once had a function in punctuation but were usurped by another, flashier symbol.

By considering what is is about symbols that has seen their use decline, it helps us to think about why we use punctuation and how its use, like the spoken language it records, is ever evolving. In earlier sections I have mentioned symbols that in modern usage, especially online, have seen their use rapidly decline. This includes the semicolon, hyphen, colon and divide symbol. Could it be that in another fifty years one or all of these symbols will have become endangered or even extinct? Well, yes. It is quite possible that instant messaging and online communication will result in a streamlining of our canon of regularly used symbols. As habits sneak into common usage, they often go on to be reflected in more formal writing.

I shall not foretell the doom of punctuation just yet; this is, after all, a book that celebrates the history and ever-changing usage of the symbols on our keyboards. However, by gathering here a selection of symbols no longer in regular use we can better understand how and why some fall out of favour and consider what has allowed others to flourish.

Tironian et

The Tironian *et* could be described as the defeated rival of the ampersand. This is because this humble symbol, which somewhat resembles the number 7, performs the same job as an ampersand, providing a single pen stroke for the Latin word *et*, meaning 'and'. Up until the Middle Ages both symbols were used as shorthand for 'and', but by the twelfth century the Tironian *et* had all but fallen out of use, in favour of its typographically more inspiring nemesis, the ampersand.

The Tironian *et* was once part of an extensive shorthand system, known as 'Tironian notes', encompassing some 14,000 symbols. This system was developed in the first century BCE by Marcus Tullius Tiro, a slave belonging to the celebrated Roman orator and statesman Cicero. One of Tiro's main duties was to record the words of Cicero for posterity. As a result he needed a system to transcribe his master's words quickly and efficiently.

Cicero was himself an admirer of the Ancient Greek shorthand system – the earliest example of which is found on the Acropolis Stone from *c.*350 BCE (held at the British Museum) – which uses a series of symbols based on the key sound of each word represented. He requested that Tiro develop something similar. The resultant shorthand was a mixture of Greek shorthand symbols and Latin abbreviations, which allowed Tiro to note down Cicero's words of wisdom, even on the move. Tiro's shorthand was much admired and was adopted by many across the ancient world. The Tironian *et* was just one of thousands of symbols in the system, but the ubiquity of the word 'and' meant it was deployed frequently. It was therefore this symbol that came to have the most widespread usage.

In the twelfth century, when fear of witchcraft and sorcery spread across Europe, writing systems based on ancient runes or used as ciphers came under suspicion. As a consequence Tironian notes fell from favour as people tried to distance themselves from anything which could be seen as remotely occult. Despite the widespread move away from Tironian notes, the Tironian *et* kept a foot in the door. As shorthand for 'and' it was adopted into most Gothic, or blackletter, fonts in the fifteenth century. But this reprieve was short-lived. As print technology improved, hard-to-read Gothic and blackletter fonts were superseded by simpler humanist fonts, which favoured the use of the ampersand. The obituary for the Tironian *et* could have been written at this time, its death knell seemingly sounded by the victory of the ampersand. However, a couple of languages held out. Irish and Scottish Gaelic retained the Tironian *et* as their chosen abbreviation for 'and'. Today this Roman relic can still be seen in the Republic of Ireland, where with space at a premium on the Irish-language side of some bilingual road signs it is deployed in place of 'and' – ensuring that, although endangered, this ancient abbreviation is yet to become extinct.

Interrobang

In typography less is more – the fewer marks on the page, the cleaner and clearer the message. This is especially true in advertising where a slogan or tagline needs to quickly impart a message with impact. In a reflection of this, in 1962 advertising executive Martin K. Speckter proposed the creation of a new symbol called the 'interrobang' to convey an excited question, incredulity or a rhetorical question. For example, you might use an interrobang at the end of the statement thus: 'You did what‽' The symbol is a combination of the question mark (forming the 'interro' part of the name, originating from one of the question mark's early names: the interrogation point) and the exclamation mark (also known by printers as a 'bang'). Prior to the invention of the interrobang an array of question marks and exclamation points had imparted a similar meaning – !? or ?! or even !??! – but this typographical clutter was deemed unseemly by Speckter, and his new symbol with the one point superimposed over the other was born.

The rhetorical question had long been a syntactical form that had confounded typographers; the interrobang was not the first symbol to attempt to convey its meaning. In 1580 English printer Henry Denham proposed using a backwards question mark to denote a rhetorical question. Denham's mark was dubbed the percontation mark, but it failed to catch on.

Speckter suggested the new symbol for use in advertising copy in 1962 in an article for the magazine *TYPEtalks*. The article generated debate about the idea of a new symbol and readers wrote in to suggest their own names for the symbol, including 'rhet', 'exclarotive' and (my personal favourite) 'exclamaquest', but Speckter stuck with 'interrobang'. Following the article the interrobang met with some success and began to appear in some modern fonts. For example, in 1966 Richard Isbell added it to his new Americana typeface for the American Type Foundry. Then in 1968 Remington Rand added the interrobang as an optional key on some of its typewriters. It seemed as if the symbol might well catch on.

But as the 1960s made way for the 1970s the interrobang fell from use, probably in part because the device was not used that often in regular writing and so failed to gain a foothold. Despite the mark not being widely adopted by the public, it can still be found in many modern typefaces, such as Wingdings 2. It also has a place in Unicode. Perhaps this mark will be revived or repurposed, like the now ubiquitous #. However, because the meaning it serves to convey is now more regularly covered by the plethora of emoji at our fingertips, it seems more likely that it will remain in obscurity.

Tilde

The tilde is a small wavy line ~ that indicates omission. It originated on the Iberian peninsula in the twelfth century and was brought into use by medieval scribes, for whom ink was expensive and space on the page at a premium. This meant that abbreviations were frequently used. In Spanish the tilde was placed over an *n* to show that there would normally be two *n*s. For example, the Latin word *annus* ('year') would be written as *año* in Spanish, saving ink and space on the page.

Over time, as the phonetic nature of Spanish became more accepted, the tilde came to represent a sound, rather than just an abbreviation of two *n*s – for example, the palatal nasal sound represented by the tilde in *piñata*. The tilde was used similarly in Portuguese on vowels to show that the letter bearing the tilde should be pronounced nasally; thus 'hand' in Latin, *manus*, became *mão* in Portuguese. In this way the original scribal mark indicating an abbreviation became indelibly linked to an *n* in Spanish and an *a* or *o* in Portuguese, the tilde less of a separate symbol than part of the letter itself, much like the dot of an *i*.

The tilde as a symbol on its own, however, came to be adopted and adapted as a mathematical symbol. In a mathematical context a tilde was used to express an inexact number; for example, 4~7 would mean that there are between 4 and 7 items; or to indicate an approximation, such as 'meet here ~15 minutes before start of lunch'. This ensured it retained a place on a standard keyboard. Although its meaning might have eluded us, its form was familiar. It was this familiarity which allowed the tilde (like the @ and the # before it) to be repurposed in the Internet age. The tilde has had a number of modern incarnations. Initially it was simply used as decoration to make an online bio look ~~~~ snazzier ~~~~. Others embraced its wave-like form by using repeated tildes to communicate a good vibe, and some (perhaps taking inspiration from the Fonz) used ~hey~ as an opening salvo in an online flirtation.

But it is on Twitter where the tilde has found a new usage, one which seems likely to rescue it from endangerment. Twitter users have been deploying the tilde around clichéd words or phrases to reclaim them or to show that they understand the word or phrase is problematic but that they are using it with self-awareness. This kind of usage implies a certain knowingness or snark. For example, a women might write about her ~sexy~ dress or caption a mundane post with ~living the dream~. The tildes serve to make the word or phrase stand out, but equally signpost that the writer is deploying that phrase or word knowingly. The use of graphemes online to convey double meanings or add flair or emphasis is ever evolving, and it is yet to be seen how enduring these new uses of endangered special characters such as the tilde will be. But right now this once obscure symbol is enjoying its time in the sun.

Hedera

The hedera (or fleuron) ❧ is named after the Latin word meaning ivy leaf, as it resembles an unfurling frond and leaf of that plant. The heart-shaped hedera is thought to be one of the oldest punctuation marks in use in the West, first appearing in Greek and Roman inscriptions from the second century BCE. In inscriptions the hedera was used as a form of punctuation, to indicate a new paragraph, in much the same way as a pilcrow does.

The hedera can also be seen in codices from the seventh and eighth centuries, where it was deployed to mark the beginning or end of a section. At some point it clearly had some function as punctuation, although, as with many of the symbols in this book, in this early period its use continued to be arbitrary. The hedera survived the introduction of the printing press – it is found indicating the opening of a paragraph or marking the start of a chapter in some sixteenth-century texts.

A number of type cutters took on the hedera and cut beautiful decorative type in its form; this may in part explain its transformation from an item of punctuation to a purely ornamental symbol. The metal type character could be rotated, so the hedera was used both vertically and horizontally, rendering it a useful and versatile glyph. Likewise with modern printing techniques it could easily be repeated in lines to form a pattern, which added decoration to a title page or a flourish to the close of a chapter. In this way the hedera became a thing of beauty rather than a workhorse of punctuation.

In Germany the hedera is known as the *Aldusblatt* after the Italian printer Aldus Manutius, who was an especial fan of the symbol and deployed it in many of his works, popularizing its use. Today it remains a familiar symbol in Germany as it is used as the logo of the publisher Hermann Schmidt. Perhaps because the hedera resembles a heart, it has been nicknamed the 'printer's heart' and continues to appear in a number of modern fonts, such as Zapf Dingbats and Minion Pro. As a piece of punctuation the hedera fell out of use hundreds of years ago, but as a decorative flourish it remains a useful symbol.

Pilcrow

¶ The pilcrow was a simple punctuation symbol used by medieval scribes to indicate the start and end of a paragraph. The concept of a paragraph was arguably the first meaningful piece of punctuation; it can be traced back to early writings in Ancient Greece. Originally blocks of text were written entirely in upper case (there was no lower case at this time) and with no spaces between the words. This created an unbroken line of text that was fiendishly hard to read. In antiquity most texts were read aloud, and so writing was a reflection of the spoken word, meaning its conventions differed from our modern formal mode of writing.

The paragraph (*paragraphos*) first appeared in writings of the fourth century BCE in Greece; it was generally represented by a horizontal line in the margin of the text. This device mostly signposted a change in subject, and signified to the reader that a significant pause should take place, so those listening to the reading would understand that the previous point had ended. A variety of typographic methods were used to highlight the change in subject (or, if a drama, the change in speaker); one common way was to mark a large capital *K*, short for *kaput* – which translates as 'head' – to show the head or start of a new argument.

By the twelfth century the *C* had taken over the job previously done by the *K*, with *C* standing for *capitulum* or chapter. Scribes used the large *C* to indicate a new section. This soon became embellished by the rubricators with horizontal lines and flourishes until it looked more like the backward *p* we recognize as a pilcrow today. Over time, instead of just indicating chapters, the pilcrow was used to show divisions of paragraphs too and soon was cropping up throughout the text. Incidentally the word 'pilcrow' is possibly itself a corruption of the word 'paragraph'. Some sources, such as the *Oxford Universal Dictionary*, suggest the word might come from 'pulled crow' due to its physical similarity to a plucked bird (though this is probably a folk etymology).

Scribes began to purposefully leave a gap in the text at the start of each new paragraph for the rubricator to fill in later with decorated (often red) pilcrows or other embellishments. When the printing press was developed and popularized in the fifteenth century, typographers originally tried to stay as faithful as possible to handwritten texts. As a consequence they too left gaps at the start of paragraphs for the rubricators to add decorated pilcrows. However, as the volume of books grew and time pressure on book printers increased there was often simply not enough time to draw in the pilcrows. This meant that many books were printed with a gap at the start of each paragraph, which was never filled by a pilcrow. Over time this absence became the accepted norm and the pilcrow became invisible. We cannot really say that the pilcrow is no longer used, because the concept persists. It is the way it is expressed that has changed, from an actual symbol to the absence of the symbol.

The pilcrow is used today as a proofreading symbol to indicate that a large chunk of text should be broken up into two paragraphs, and also as shorthand in legal texts to denote a numbered paragraph (as in ¶6). Furthermore, the pilcrow can be found as a 'button' in modern word-processing programs such as Word, where when 'switched on' it will make all punctuation and spaces visible for the typesetter. This modern word-processing pilcrow is a non-permanent mark – meaning that it does not show up in print but does perform a function. And so the pilcrow is not entirely defunct. However, the pilcrow is today an invisible punctuation mark: the gap where it once stood continues to communicate a new paragraph, but its actual presence is not needed.

Manicule

A manicule ☞ (also known as a fist) is a small, originally hand-drawn, picture of a hand with three fingers clenched and the index finger pointing, sometimes emerging from a cuff. The word 'manicule' derives from the Latin *maniculum*, meaning 'little hand'. The first known use of a manicule was in the Domesday Book of 1086; it began appearing more regularly from the twelfth century.

Rather than being a punctuation mark added by the writer or scribe to clarify the text, the manicule is more frequently scrawled by readers, making their own annotations to a book – highlighting important passages, indicating new paragraphs or pointing to a part of the text taken from a different source. In this way the manicule represented a dialogue between the reader and the writer, the hand-drawn annotation revealing their unique relationship to the text.

Manicules became especially popular in fourteenth- and fifteenth-century Italy and can be found in numerous texts, each rendering unique to the creator. Some are just a simple line drawing; others show great flair and detail with carefully drawn fingernails and elaborate cuffs. Archbishop Matthew Parker (1504–1575) was especially fond of the manicule; many of the books in his collection, which was bequeathed to Corpus Christi College Library in Cambridge, are peppered with manicules, providing palaeographers with enticing clues as to his relationship with the books and his views on the importance of certain passages. The use of manicules is especially interesting because it takes time to draw them – why not use a simple arrow to draw attention to the text? Professor William H. Sherman, one of the foremost experts on the manicule, observes that the device represents an actual gesture, and therefore it holds more weight than a simple arrow or asterisk might.

After the introduction of the printing press, hand-drawn manicules continued to appear in book margins, indicating that readers were still keen to customize their own books. But by the eighteenth and nineteenth centuries the habit seemed to be fading from use, just as the number of printed manicules flourished. In the nineteenth century type cutters began to create more and more versions of the manicule, including the one still most frequently seen today – the pointing hand emerging from the neat white cuff of a black business suit. Printers began to deploy these printed manicules directly in the text to highlight chapter titles or subtitles, to break the text into subsections, or at the bottom of the page to indicate that the text continues overleaf. As manicules became more commonly printed they began to creep into industrial contexts and were used in advertising, pointing to key information. It is this context in which we most often see manicules used today, bringing a vintage flavour to an advert or as a kooky bullet point. Although this iteration still holds on to the original idea of highlighting key points in the text, it has lost its conversational mode, as now it is the advertiser telling us what is important, rather than the readers themselves interacting with the text and noting their own thoughts.

Today scrawling directly in a book is frowned upon, and so we have fallen out of the habit of drawing manicules beside passages we find of especial interest. The option now exists, of course, to deploy the neon highlighter pen on texts to perform the same function as the pilcrow, but minus the personality. The symbol, though, lives on in the digital world, the computer cursor transforming itself from an arrow to a pointing hand when we hover over a link that takes us off to another web page. The symbol of a hand, representing our physical relationship with holding, pointing, taking, continues to provide a link between the reader and the written word.

> Mathematics is the language
> with which God wrote the Universe.
>
> *Galileo*

> I am incapable of conceiving infinity,
> and yet I do not accept finity.
>
> *Simone de Beauvoir*

> Perfection is attained by slow degrees;
> it requires the hand of time.
>
> *Voltaire*

Further reading

Blatt, Ben, *Nabokov's Favorite Word is Mauve*, Simon & Schuster, New York, 2017.

Bringhurst, Robert, *Elements of Typographic Style*, Hartley & Marks, Vancouver, 1992.

Burton, David M., *The History of Mathematics: An Introduction*, 7th edn, McGraw-Hill, New York, 2011.

Cajori, Florian, *A History of Mathematical Notations*, Dover Publications, New York, 1993.

Caneva, Adriana, Anna Davies and Shiro Nishimoto, *Glyph: A Visual Exploration of Punctuation Marks and Other Typographic Symbols*, Cicada Books, London, 2015.

Chrisomalis, Stephen, *Numerical Notation: A Comparative History*, Cambridge University Press, Cambridge, 2010.

Crystal, David, *Making a Point: The Pernickety Story of English Punctuation*, Profile Books, London, 2015.

Davies, Glyn, *A History of Money from Ancient Times to the Present Day*, 3rd edn, University of Wales Press, Cardiff, 2002.

Houston, Keith, *Shady Characters: Ampersands, Interrobangs and other Typographical Curiosities*, Particular Books, London, 2013.

Ifrah, Georges, *From One to Zero: A Universal History of Numbers* trans. Lowell Bair, Viking, New York, 1985.

Mazur, Joseph, *Enlightening Symbols: A Short History of Mathematical Notation and Its Hidden Powers*, Princeton University Press, Princeton NJ, 2014.

Parkes, M.B., *Pause and Effect: An Introduction to the History of Punctuation in the West*, Scolar Press, London, 1992.

Sherman, William H., 'Toward a History of the Manicule', www.livesandletters.ac.uk/papers/for_2005_04_001.pdf, March 2005.

Toner, Anne, *Ellipsis in English Literature: Signs of Omission*, Cambridge University Press, Cambridge, 2015.

Tschichold, Jan, *A Brief History of the Ampersand*, trans. Jean-Marie Clarke, Zeug, Paris, 2017.

Index